© 2020 Writt

Cover Art Le Printemps (
Used under Open Source CC0 1.0 Universal Publ

Cover Graphic Design by Avi Yiska Epstein

Scripture quotations marked (NIV) are taken from, and unless otherwise indicated, all Scripture quotations are taken from THE HOLY BIBLE, NEW INTERNATIONAL VERSION®, NIV® Copyright © 1973, 1978, 1984, 2011 by Biblica, Inc.® Used by permission. All rights reserved worldwide.

Scripture quotations marked (BSB) are taken from The Holy Bible, Berean Study Bible, BSB Copyright ©2016, 2018 by Bible Hub Used by Permission. All Rights Reserved Worldwide.

Scripture quotations marked (ABPE) are taken from the ARAMAIC BIBLE IN PLAIN ENGLISH, 2010 Copyright©, Rev. David Bauscher, Lulu Enterprises Incorporated, 2010.

Scripture quotations marked (NKJV) are taken from the NEW KING JAMES VERSION®. Copyright© 1982 by Thomas Nelson, Inc. Used by permission. All rights reserved.

Scripture quotations marked (YLT) are taken from the 1898 YOUNG'S LITERAL TRANSLATION OF THE HOLY BIBLE by J.N. Young, (Author of the Young's Analytical Concordance), public domain.

This book is published as The Passover Season approaches. People are staying indoors because an unexpected Sabbath is coming on America, which took no Sabbaths. It is the midst of the Fast of Lent.

Our prayer is for the God of Israel to shelter America under His Passover as the people of the land repent during this time of Sabbath, and as we fast for a New Day of righteousness to dawn in America.

DISCLAIMER

This book is written and produced for informational purposes only. It is not medical advice or instruction, medical nutrition therapy, or nutrition counseling.

Statements within this book have not been evaluated or approved by the U.S. Food and Drug Administration. No content in this book is intended to diagnose, treat, cure, or prevent any disease. Book content should not be considered a substitute for professional medical expertise or treatment.

All opinions and thoughts shared through this book are purely our own. The information we share is based on our own experiences and information we learned from our own research. We are not prescribing supplements, specific dietary plans, formulating menus, or recommending web sites in any links. Please consult a qualified health care professional regarding health conditions or concerns, and before starting a new diet or health or exercise program or taking any supplements.

CHAPTER 1 WHY WE WROTE THIS BOOK

A few months ago when the whole coronavirus thing started appearing in the news, we were reading about the coronavirus starting to affect people in Asia.

Naturally our first thought is to protect our family from any danger.

We already eat healthy, and we talked about how different natural foods and remedies might be helpful in times of plague.

We began reading, and making notes of things.

We read some research studies on the internet. We tried to think about different ideas we found and thought made sense to us that might be helpful to prevent disease, and made notes about those.

We found, for example -

- There are at least four different kinds of influenza found in the U.S., and they change and mutate every year.
- There are seven different types of coronavirus
- More than 200 types of viruses can cause a cold

We realized that *we need to go on a war footing against all kinds of viruses all the time*, not just the latest plague.

We found that two *very simple* remedies, which are both time tested, and lab science proven - kill every virus known to man. Here they are -

> **Gargle salt water (including irrigation of the nose)**
>
> **Garlic**
>
> **Besides those, there are at least a couple dozen other natural herbs and substances which appear to fight viruses. Some of them specifically act against various types of coronaviruses.**

You'll find details and links to the research studies we found, later in this book.

We think a problem is that many people don't <u>**act ahead of time.**</u>

Laying in bed with pneumonia is not the time to start gargling salt water and using garlic.

The point is to kill viruses before they get started. At least that's the way we see it.

You can get tested if you think you have symptoms of coronavirus. But we feel we'd rather be using things that are known to fight or kill viruses *before* there are any symptoms. You can't see a virus where it is, so you don't know if one landed somewhere. That's why people are wiping down tables and other surfaces, and washing their hands. Those are good things to do. But if a virus may have landed in someone's nose or throat, it makes sense to us to use something that can kill it, even if it's not even there. Better safe than sorry. Why wait until there are symptoms to do something?

Again, that's just our personal opinion and take on things. We do everything the CDC, WHO, UNICEF, and doctors are recommending to do.

Then we are personally adding natural herbal remedies to those things. We are not recommending that anyone else do what we're doing. In case you want to know about those things, that's why we wrote this book. We put this where you can read it in the preview so you can decide whether you feel you want to buy the book.

In this book we are reporters and we are offering our notes and thoughts as a reference for those who might want to use them as a jumping off place to do their own research and come to their own conclusions.

If you want to use some of these ideas, please do your own research and come to your own conclusions. What works for us may not work for you.

This is no medical advice in this book and we are not physicians nor are we medical professionals. We are just regular people trying to understand what's happening in the world.

So while we hope the information in this book is helpful to you, please CONSULT YOUR DOCTOR if you are ill or if you want authoritative medical advice.

Ways That God Heals

To us, prayer based on the actual promises in the Scriptures is the #1 thing to do in the End Times, for this plague and all other plagues, for whatever you need, spiritual, physical, relationship, financial, etc. Seek first the Kingdom of God, and ***all these things*** will be given to you by God.

But also don't neglect common sense and advice from doctors.

There are a lot of Bible verses in our book. We dug out verses that speak to us about God's healing and protection, and we hope they bless you also.

We give our thoughts on Scripture and hope they will inspire you.

We believe that God has given Woman gifts of healing and a ministry of healing that has been largely overlooked by the church in America today.

Later in the book we list **7 Ways that Woman Brings Healing** to her Man and to her family.

We believe God for healing. We know He heals.

However, sometimes God uses doctors and medical personnel for healing too.

Some may say that's a "lack of faith" to use doctors. Well everyone has their own opinion.

At the end of the book, you'll find the first section of Scriptures is titled "Healing Ministry of Jesus the Messiah". There you can read about healing miracles that Yeshua (Jesus) did, which included -

- a blind man
- a paralyzed man
- a woman with an issue of blood

> lepers

> sick people who were laying in the street

> two people who had died

All these healings happened instantly.

Those were all miracles of healing that only God can perform.

Yet, we find that Yeshua also did the following healing miracles -

> *He healed multitudes that had become ill with various diseases and he cast out many evil spirits.*

> Yeshua traveled through all Galilee and he taught in their assemblies and preached the Good News of the Kingdom and *cured every sickness and disease among the people*.

> His fame was heard in all Syria, and *they brought to him all those who had become ill with various diseases, those who were afflicted with severe pain, and the demon possessed, and lunatics and paralytics, and he healed them all.*

Clearly, Yeshua healed *all diseases*, from the worst ones, to probably sore throats and common colds. Whatever people needed, He headed them - including if they were tormented with demons, or had mental challenges.

He healed them all.

Yet He did not rebuke the woman with the issue of blood for going to see doctors.

We believe that healing is good, period.

Healing from the Hand of God is the best.

Sometimes God heals us instantly.

Sometimes God gives us gradual healing.

Sometimes we have to knock at His door daily and tell Him we are not going to leave Him alone until He gives us our healing.

But healing from doctors is a good thing also. We are grateful for the many people in the medical professions who have dedicated their lives to healing and to the fight against disease.

We also believe strongly that *preventing* disease is the best of all. Better to not need healing in the first place.

It's good to pray for divine health from God. And while praying for that, we put things in our mouths that do not interfere with God answering that prayer, but which promote the health of the body.

Yet there are a lot of people in churches eating fast food and worse, who come up to the altar for healing again and again.

We think it's better to *prevent* disease in the first place, than to need healing.

That's where herbal and other natural remedies make sense to us.

We also think that God can use any means He wants to deliver us, like the Pastor who was stranded in this famous joke told by Joel Osteen -

> A big storm came into a town and local officials sent out an emergency warning that the riverbanks would soon overflow and flood the nearby homes. They ordered everyone in the town to evacuate immediately.
>
> A Pastor heard the warning and decided to stay, saying to himself, "I will trust God and if I am in danger, then God will send a divine miracle to save me."
>
> The neighbors came by his house and said to him, "We're leaving and there is room for you in our car, please come with us!" But the man declined. "I have faith that God will save me." So the car drove away.
>
> As the man stood on his porch watching the water rise up the steps, a man in a canoe paddled by and called to him, "Hurry and come into my canoe, the waters are rising quickly!" But the man again said, "No thanks, God will save me." So the canoe went on.

The floodwaters rose higher pouring water into his living room and the man had to retreat to the second floor. A police motorboat came by and saw him at the window. "We will come up and rescue you!" they shouted. But the man refused, waving them off saying, "Use your time to save someone else! I have faith that God will save me!" So the motorboat went on.

The flood waters rose higher and higher and the man had to climb up to his rooftop.

A helicopter spotted him and dropped a rope ladder. A rescue officer came down the ladder and pleaded with the man, "Grab my hand and I will pull you up!" But the man still refused, "No thank you! I'm praying to God and he is going to save me." So the helicopter flew away.

Shortly after, the house broke up and the floodwaters swept the man away. He arrives at the gates of heaven and says to St. Peter, I thought God would grant me a miracle and I have been let down." St. Peter responds, "I don't know what you're complaining about, we sent you a car, two boats, and a helicopter."

Two Key Things For Times Like This

The bible says -

Fear not

Get understanding

We decided to take a 'no panic' approach. In order to build our faith, we began scouring the bible for promises of Protection that God has given us.

For understanding, we began sifting through news articles on the internet, looking for nuggets that might help us to get a clearer picture of what was happening, and what we personally thought we might be able to do about it.

Our goal was to see what we could learn about how to protect ourselves and our family.

We've always been focused on eating healthy, because we read somewhere that 75% of all hospital visits have something to do with food.

This book tells about what we decided to do after reading what we found over the past few months.

We are not giving advice to anyone, we are just doing kind of a reality book about how we eat with the goal to prevent disease, in hopes that it will inspire other people to do their own research and come to their own conclusions about what might be good for them.

We're describing the process we have gone through -

Fear Not

Get Understanding

...and *that* process we *do* recommend to everyone, because it's two of the ways that the Kingdom of God works. The Kingdom involves many ways, but these two seem appropriate right now.

If you go through the process of abandoning fear, and getting as much understanding that you can, we believe God will show you the best paths to take. *That's the purpose of this book*, to encourage you to do those two things.

We are regular people, we are not physicians or medical professionals. We believe what the bible says, and try to do what it says. We are learning all the time.

People have said that the information found on the internet is at least 45% false. Maybe it's more than that.

So like us, please take the samples of internet info in this book with a grain of salt - literally. We're basically acting as news reporters about what we've read on the internet, this book is something like a blog post. It might give you an idea of what's out there on the internet, but you'll have to do your own reading to see if you agree or disagree. We are sure there's lots more information we didn't find yet.

We don't claim to have any medical, dietician, or other expertise, we're just trying to get through this like everybody else.

Living In The End Times

Lots of people in many churches today love hearing about living in the End Times - until the End Times start showing up at their front door.

We have included in the last part of the book some verses about Healing, Protection, and Deliverance, which seem to apply very well to the End Times. Jesus predicted everything a couple thousand years ago. Nothing today is a surprise to God.

And you should not fear anything today, because God has been protecting His people in bad situations for thousands of years.

Plagues are annoying, to say the least. But God can heal any plague. And, better than healing - is prevention. Better to never get a plague in the first place.

That's what we've been thinking about, what could we do, what could we eat, that might help prevent getting coronavirus (or any other plague) in the first place.

This book will tell you what *we're* doing. It is *not* a recommendation for what you should do, which might be completely different from what we're doing. We're not giving you medical advice in any way - if you want or need medical advice CONSULT A DOCTOR right away.

Like everyone else, we have no idea if the information on the internet is accurate or complete. We don't know if what we're doing for ourselves will work, but we hope so.

And we know that we should GET UNDERSTANDING. And we believe DO NOT FEAR, at all times.

This is what the bible says:

> **Luke 12.32 Do not be afraid, fear not.**
>
> **Isaiah 35.4 Be strong, do not fear; your God will come.**
>
> **Proverbs 4.7 Wisdom is the main thing. Therefore get wisdom. And with all your getting, get understanding.**
>
> **Proverbs 19.8 The one who gets wisdom loves life; the one who cherishes understanding will soon prosper.**

Find out everything you can, pray over it, then make your own decisions about what you will do.

No matter what happens, we do know these things are true -

> God protects His people in all ages and in all circumstances.
>
> God gives wisdom and understanding to those who seek it and to those who ask Him
>
> If nothing works and the world ends, then His people will be with Him in Heaven, which will be better anyway.

In the meantime, we go about our business, and trust in God, because God is the only real Refuge and Shelter in this world.

CHAPTER 2 FOLK REMEDIES WE FOUND THAT SCIENCE VALIDATES

Genesis 1.11-12 Then God said, "Let the earth bring forth vegetation: seed-bearing plants and fruit trees, each bearing fruit with seed according to its kind." And it was so. The earth produced vegetation: seed-bearing plants according to their kinds and trees bearing fruit with seed according to their kinds. And God saw that it was good.

The Garden of Eden knew no war, disease, greed, treachery, or hatred. All those things came after Man and Woman fell.

From that time until now, human history has been punctuated by wars and plagues.

The Hebrew bible says that the Last Days will just have more of those things.

Yet God knows how to keep and protect those who belong to Him.

Just as He made clothes from animals to clothe Adam and Eve, we believe He has provided simple, natural ways to help us deal with things like the coronavirus plague that's in the news right now.

We believe He put plants and trees on earth that have healing properties. It's well known that giant pharmaceutical companies scour the Amazon rain forest and test rare plants for healing compounds. Those plants and compounds were created by God for us to learn about and use.

God has also provided great talent to doctors and researchers to find cures and remedies for diseases. We believe that the medical community is part of God's plan of healing for Man and Woman.

Luke who wrote one of the four books of the New Testament, was a physician.

We pray for God to grant wisdom, stamina, courage, and serenity to all the medical professionals on earth curing people during this time of plague.

The bible contains over a hundred promises about healing and divine protection, which we've set out in the last chapter of this book for you to read and meditate wherever there is a need.

Ultimately, those who call on the Messiah of Israel will join Him in Heaven one day, where the Garden of Eden will be restored in a New Heaven and a New Jerusalem. All sorrow and sighing will flee away.

How Do You Stop A Cold Before It Gets Started?

We were thinking about that question.

We were wondering is there a folk remedy that we could use and maybe help prevent ever getting coronavirus (and other plagues)? We couldn't find anything like that in most news articles.

But it might be that different cultures have been using methods like this for a thousand years to prevent disease.

Our process leading up to this book has been to -

> Reduce Panic.
>
>> The news media may not now it, but the God of Israel is still on the Throne.
>>
>> We want to keep our heads while others are losing theirs.
>
> Get Understanding.
>
>> It turns out that natural and herbal antiviral remedies exist that have been known for thousands of years, and have no doubt killed trillions of viruses over the centuries. We wondered has science confirmed any of them? Would we want to use them?
>
> Study the Healing Ministry of the Woman in all ages.
>
>> So many people never go to hospital because a Woman kept disease away from them. Some end up in hospital because a Woman was absent from the place where she could minister healing to them.
>>
>> We wanted to find out about any simple, inexpensive, easy to learn remedies and routines which will hopefully improve our wellness through food, and which may help keep us from catching viruses and other dis-

eases.

Keep a balanced perspective.

For all the amazing chemicals, drugs, and equipment that modern medicine has brought, we thought maybe there are still foods and remedies that God sent in ages past which are good for all time. We read that studies have found that some natural therapies appear to equal the best that modern medicine can do. According to some research studies a few of them actually exceed anything that modern science has discovered so far, such as garlic. We are not against science at all - anything that brings healing is good. But we didn't want to throw out what has worked since ancient times, if it can still work.

We want to live in good health and blessing. We're sure most people want that too. We started doing some things different after we began our "End Times survival project".

A Common Sense Remedy that Mom Knew About

When we read the newspapers, we saw that -

- The coronavirus can spread through the air.
- It lodges in the throat tissue.
- People can have it for a week or two and not know it.

Public health pronouncements have included -
- Wash your hands
- Cover your coughs and sneezes
- Stay at home from work or school if you have symptoms.

- Avoid crowds.

- You see notices like, "Officials urged residents to stay calm and take precautions recommended nationally: Wash hands frequently, avoid crowds, stay home when sick, and avoid contact with ill people."

That's all great advice. But we wondered -

> What if people are breathing or touching viruses they don't even know are there?

> Because some people show no symptoms.

In other words, it's hard for someone to avoid ill people if no one is aware they are ill.

It's also hard for someone to "stay home when sick" if they don't know they're sick.

People could have viruses landing in their nose, then on to their throat, and not realize it.

So it seemed to us just common sense that it might not hurt to assume that there could be unknown viruses that should be killed, even if someone is not sure they're there or not.

We remember our mothers telling us to "gargle salt water" at the first sign of a sore throat or sniffle.

We listened, and we avoided a lot of colds, flu, and viruses that were "going around".

So we have started gargling salt water every day at least a couple times, and more at night - even though we have no symptoms of anything.

We figure it can't hurt.

What we did not know when we started making this part of our daily routine is that -

- **The cells of our body can use Salt to kill viruses.**
- **Gargling salt water can actually speed up recovery from colds, which might be sometimes caused by a virus with some similarity to the coronavirus.**
- **That's because gargling salt water can kill viruses in the throat, which the coronavirus uses as a "staging area" to multiply, often before a person even knows the virus is there.**
- **Irrigating the nose with salt water can start killing viruses before they even get to the throat.**

Here are links to the research study that says this, read it for yourself:

https://www.scotsman.com/news-2-15012/scientists-believe-salt-could-be-cure-to-common-cold-1-4865207

https://www.scotsman.com/news-2-15012/scientists-believe-salt-could-be-cure-to-common-cold-1-4865207

http://www.elvisstudy.com

http://www.elvisstudy.com/nasal-irrigation-and-gargling.html

https://www.nature.com/articles/s41598-018-37703-3

https://www.nature.com/articles/s41598-018-31936-y

So here's what common sense might suggest at this time -

- If no one knows if they were even exposed to the coronavirus, why not start killing any viruses that might be in the nose by irrigating with salt water.
- Why not start killing viruses that might be in the throat by gargling with salt water.

- If a person has not been exposed to the coronavirus, no harm done.

- But if they have been exposed, and don't know it - then they hopefully may have started killing coronavirus before it gets started.

While we're at it, we wanted to start eating foods that are said to help kill viruses in general.

There is a list of some of those foods in this book, along with the lab research supporting their effectiveness.

Nobody wants to wait in a crowded hospital with sick people and get tested for coronavirus.

Nobody wants to end up in a hospital bed being treated with expensive and powerful chemical drugs if they don't have to.

Will salt water and natural remedies prevent coronavirus? No one knows, but it sure can't hurt. We personally want to use anything and everything reasonable that might help us.

It's cheap to use salt water and natural foods. If it does work on only a few people, it will have been well worth it. If a lot of people find help that way, it will save vast amounts of suffering, anxiety, and money.

Even if someone uses these natural remedies but gets coronavirus anyway, maybe it will be a weaker version, or maybe they will get over it sooner because they are killing germs in their throat the whole time. No one knows yet because doctors are still learning about the coronavirus.

Do what your doctor tells you. But that doesn't mean leaving out the remedies Dr. Jesus has put in natural substances on the earth which have helped people for millennia. Ask your doctor about anything you want to try, especially if you are already taking medications for anything else or if you have other health issues.

Sometimes simple is better. Remember when bread in the US went through several "steps" to "refine" the flour - including hybridizing the wheat plant? Did you ever read the list of "modern" bread "ingredients" which sometimes contained dozens of chemicals? After eating that "bread" did your stomach ever feel like you ate a bowling ball?

Then someone had the idea of baking bread with unrefined, non-hybridized flour, water, salt, and yeast. It tasted way better, and digested better. Oh, and that's how bread was made for thousands of years before "modern" complicated "ideas" came along of how to make bread "better". The "modern" part certainly made a lot of chemical companies rich.

Our "modern" society sometimes overcomplicates things that only need to be simple.

Salt water and some very cheap natural remedies, if they work or not, are an investment we are making at this time.

The Woman's Ancient, But Now Forgotten Role of Healer

In this book we discuss Woman's ancient, but now largely forgotten role in healing and health. We believe Women have a ministry that could reduce or eliminate most hospital visits for their families. There is science for this also, the research on the people of Ikaria.

Treasury of Healing, Protection, and Deliverance Scriptures

At the end of the book we've included tables of Scriptures you can quickly turn to any time you need a Word from the Spirit of God for healing, or protection from plague or other danger, or deliverance from trouble.

This handy reference is in the last section of the book, so you can keep it on your living room table or by your bed and easily turn to it at any time.

There is space provided near each Scripture where you can write down answers to prayer you received, insights you received from God, and notes.

CHAPTER 3 WE THOUGHT HOW CAN WE FIGHT THE PLAGUE?

The Chinese have some of the very best top medical talent in the world. Soon 400 million people were locked down in quarantine in an all out effort to contain the coronavirus.

Yet despite best efforts, the coronavirus continued to spread, and new cases were found around the world, including the US.

Powerful antiviral drugs have been used to try and stop it, and some limited tests had encouraging results.

People began to panic in some areas.

If you're a believer, you know that God was not caught by surprise by this plague.

He has provided us all things - spiritual and physical - for every situation we could ever face, and this is no exception.

Do you remember when you were a kid and you got a cold?

Your mother had a simple answer: gargle salt water every 30 minutes until your throat stopped hurting.

Then keep gargling day and night until the cold went away.

Maybe your mother also fed you food sprinkled with raw garlic.

She knew what modern science has confirmed.

Both salt water and garlic are known to kill all sorts of viruses.

There are clinical studies which now prove this.

<u>Garlic is a natural virus killer.</u>

>https://www.ncbi.nlm.nih.gov/pubmed/29023413

<u>Gargling salt water kills cold viruses.</u>

It seems that God had already given part of the answer to scientists not long ago at the University of Edinburgh, Scotland -

>https://www.scotsman.com/news-2-15012/scientists-believe-salt-could-be-cure-to-common-cold-1-4865207

>http://www.elvisstudy.com

>http://www.elvisstudy.com/nasal-irrigation-and-gargling.html

>https://www.nature.com/articles/s41598-018-37703-3

>https://www.nature.com/articles/s41598-018-31936-y

The research project run by the University of Edinburgh published in January 2019 found that salt kills all types of viruses.

People's cells use chloride ions from the salt to make hypochlorous acid - which is the active ingredient found in bleach.

Cells basically use the chloride ion to make bleach to get rid of viral infections – because bleach kills all viruses. Bleach is what many hospitals used to kill the aids virus and disinfect trays, toilets, floors, etc.

After my mother told me to gargle salt water for a cold, my father told me to dip my pinkie in the salt water and gently put the salt water up my nose. Just dip it, put it in, then repeat for the other nostril. Gently, don't breathe it in, he said, just lightly wet the inside of your nose on both sides with salt water. Do it every time you gargle.

Irrigating your nose with salt water has been recorded in ancient texts that are thousands of years old.

We have not read many news stories which mention either of these tried and true remedies for a cold virus, although the coronavirus appears to be a bad cousin to the family of cold viruses.

Coronavirus is similar to a mild cold in some patients, and is more like the flu in other patients. According to news reports, the coronavirus is a member of the class of cold and flu viruses. Reports are that it has a characteristic that makes it more contagious than other similar bad viruses.

So why haven't we heard about this simple idea?

In fact, gargling with salt water was commonly recommended by doctors in Europe as well as the US, up until the First World War. It seems to have become an "old wives tale" after antibiotics were invented.

Yet antibiotics cannot kill viruses. Antibiotics kill bacteria.

The US Centers for Disease Control (CDC) itself says, "Antibiotics do not work on viruses."

   https://www.cdc.gov/features/antibioticuse/index.html

The new study from Scotland (above) shows that our cells need the chloride ion from salt to stop viruses from multiplying.

The really good news is that the study says this mechanism works against all types of viruses.

Common sense would tell you that it can't hurt to gargle salt water and irrigate your nose with salt water just like my mother and father told me, while waiting for the plague of coronavirus to be contained by the public health authorities.

Some people even mix an iodine solution with salt water for nasal rinses because "Iodine is a deadly enemy of single-cell micro-organisms" -

>   https://www.dmrpublications.com/2014/08/lets-kill-super-bugs/

Another option might be a Neti pot. Jala Neti (nasal irrigation with salt water) has been recorded in ancient texts that are thousands of years old.

Steam could be good too.

Garlic Kills Viruses and Bacteria

In America, there are many couples who have agreed not to eat garlic, because one of them doesn't like the smell.

On the other hand, if you're from Eastern Europe as my wife is, you probably know that people who eat a lot of raw garlic rarely get sick.

Why is that?

Diallylthiosulfinate (Allicin), a volatile antimicrobial from garlic kills human lung pathogenic bacteria, including multi-drug resistant strains.

>   https://www.ncbi.nlm.nih.gov/pubmed/29023413

In other words, even when antibiotics quit working, garlic can still kill those bacteria. God created garlic for us, and it's better than the strongest antibiotics, because garlic works even when they don't.

Science says that something called "MSM" may generally make your body work better.

Around 1965, chemists began investigating MSM, a stable, cheap, organic sulphur compound with medicinal properties, a form of which is found in garlic -

> https://www.healthleadsuk.com/msm-miracle/

> https://en.wikipedia.org/wiki/Methylsulfonylmethane

CHAPTER 4 HERBS AND PLANT EXTRACTS WHICH CAN HELP FIGHT VIRUSES

Genesis 1.11-12 Then God said, "Let the earth bring forth vegetation: seed-bearing plants and fruit trees, each bearing fruit with seed according to its kind." And it was so. The earth produced vegetation: seed-bearing plants according to their kinds and trees bearing fruit with seed according to their kinds. <u>*And God saw that it was good*</u>.

God knew long ago that we would need healing from plagues and other problems.

So He created plants and trees with healing properties. He saw that it was good that He had created them.

Some of these natural remedies have been used for hundreds or even thousands of years to treat virus infections.

Remember, garlic works against viruses. But antibiotics only work against bacteria, not viruses.

Some of these natural medicines have been found by research to attack viruses somewhat like the coronavirus. But not all of these have been thoroughly researched, so do your own homework.

Herbs and Plant Extracts That Can Help Fight Viruses

Herb	Against which viruses has it been found effective?	Research and Notes
Astragalus	*avian influenza H9 viruses*	https://www.ncbi.nlm.nih.gov/pubmed/30772802
		https://www.ncbi.nlm.nih.gov/pmc/articles/PMC3729712/
		https://www.ncbi.nlm.nih.gov/pmc/articles/PMC4663710/
	also herpes, hepatitis C	https://www.ncbi.nlm.nih.gov/pmc/articles/PMC4098889/
		https://www.ncbi.nlm.nih.gov/pubmed/14724098
Basil (Sweet)	*enterovirus* (which causes symptoms similar to colds)	Antiviral activities of extracts and selected pure constituents of sweet basil.
		https://www.ncbi.nlm.nih.gov/pubmed/16173941
	also herpes, hepatitis B	
Basil (Holy)	*Increased levels of helper T cells and natural killer cells, both are immune cells that help the body kill viruses	https://www.ncbi.nlm.nih.gov/pubmed/21619917
Cat's Claw	Inhibition of viral attachment in the host cells was the main mechanism of antiviral activity.	https://www.ncbi.nlm.nih.gov/pubmed/24447975
	Antiviral in vitro effects displayed novel properties and might be further investigated as a promising candidate for clinical application.	https://www.ncbi.nlm.nih.gov/pubmed/18279801
Dandelion	*influenza*	https://www.ncbi.nlm.nih.gov/pubmed/22168277
	hepatitis B, HIV	https://www.ncbi.nlm.nih.gov/pubmed/22078030
		https://www.ncbi.nlm.nih.gov/pubmed/24481875

	May also inhibit replication of some viruses	https://www.ncbi.nlm.nih.gov/pmc/articles/PMC5857124/
		https://www.ncbi.nlm.nih.gov/books/NBK430732/
Echinacea	*colds and influenza*	https://www.ncbi.nlm.nih.gov/pmc/articles/PMC4058675/
	herpes	https://www.ncbi.nlm.nih.gov/pmc/articles/PMC4058675/
	Used by Native Americans to fight viruses	https://www.ncbi.nlm.nih.gov/pubmed/22131823
Elderberry (Sambucus nigra) (Sambucol)	Elderberry supplements found to substantially reduce upper respiratory symptoms caused by viruses including the *flu* and *common cold*	https://www.ncbi.nlm.nih.gov/pubmed/30670267
	concentrated elderberry juice suppressed influenza virus replication and stimulated immune system response	https://www.ncbi.nlm.nih.gov/pubmed/22972323
	Inhibited replication of human *influenza* viruses	https://www.ncbi.nlm.nih.gov/pubmed/9395631
Fennel	*parainfluenza* type-3 (PI-3), which causes respiratory infections in cattle	https://www.ncbi.nlm.nih.gov/pmc/articles/PMC4137549/
	herpes	https://www.ncbi.nlm.nih.gov/pubmed/20008902
	Anti-inflammatory effects	https://www.ncbi.nlm.nih.gov/pmc/articles/PMC4342739/
Garlic	human papillomavirus (HPV)	https://onlinelibrary.wiley.com/doi/abs/10.1111/j.1365-4632.2004.02348.x
	eliminated all HPV warts after 2 weeks	https://www.ncbi.nlm.nih.gov/pmc/articles/PMC1764803/
	viral pneumonia, and *rhinovirus*, which causes the *common cold*	https://www.ncbi.nlm.nih.gov/pmc/articles/PMC4103721/
	influenza A and B	https://www.ncbi.nlm.nih.gov/pmc/articles/PMC4103721/
	HIV, HSV-1	https://www.ncbi.nlm.nih.gov/pmc/articles/PMC4103721/
	Also enhances immune system response, stimulates immune cells which kill viruses	https://www.ncbi.nlm.nih.gov/pmc/articles/PMC4417560/

Ginger	*avian influenza, Respiratory syncytial virus (RSV)*	https://www.ncbi.nlm.nih.gov/pubmed/29039335
		https://www.ncbi.nlm.nih.gov/pubmed/23123794
	feline calicivirus (FCV) which is *comparable to human norovirus*	https://www.ncbi.nlm.nih.gov/pubmed/27296605
	Article on Swine Flu shows Ginger inhibits virus replication and prevents viruses from entering host cells	https://www.ncbi.nlm.nih.gov/pmc/articles/PMC2957173/
Ginseng	Coxsackievirus (respiratory illness, including sore throat, cough, and malaise (feeling tired)	https://www.ncbi.nlm.nih.gov/pmc/articles/PMC5052424/
	Also inhibits: RSV, herpes viruses, hepatitis A, hepatitis B, and norovirus	https://www.ncbi.nlm.nih.gov/pmc/articles/PMC4072342/
		https://www.ncbi.nlm.nih.gov/pubmed/23717174
		https://www.ncbi.nlm.nih.gov/pmc/articles/PMC5052424/
Green Tea	*Influenza virus* Also inhibits these viruses: HBV, HSV, EBV, Adenovirus, HIV, HCV, DENV, JEV,TBEV, ZIKV, CHIKV, HTLV-1, Rotavirus, Enterovirus, EV71, EBOV, PRRSV, VHSV, IHNV, SVCV, and GCRV	https://www.ncbi.nlm.nih.gov/pmc/articles/PMC6152177/
Hesperetin (the predominant flavonoid in lemons and oranges)	Test tube activity against SARS-CoV coronavirus.	https://www.ncbi.nlm.nih.gov/pubmed/16597209
Houttuynia cordata (aka Chinese lizard tail, or Bishop's weed)	Exhibited significant inhibitory effects on SARS-CoV coronavirus.	https://www.ncbi.nlm.nih.gov/pubmed/18479853
Isatis indigotica (woad aka Asp of Jerusalem)	Anti-SARS coronavirus effects	https://www.ncbi.nlm.nih.gov/pubmed/16115693
Lemon balm	avian influenza (bird flu), herpes viruses, HIV-1, and enterovirus 71	Aqueous extracts from peppermint, sage, and lemon balm leaves display potent anti-HIV-1 activity by increasing the virion density. https://www.ncbi.nlm.nih.gov/pmc/articles/PMC2288616/

	Also see:	https://www.ncbi.nlm.nih.gov/pmc/articles/PMC4908999/
		https://www.ncbi.nlm.nih.gov/pubmed/18693101
		https://www.ncbi.nlm.nih.gov/pubmed/24817544
		https://www.ncbi.nlm.nih.gov/pmc/articles/PMC5613005/
Licorice	***Severe acute respiratory syndrome-related coronavirus* (SARS-CoV)	https://www.ncbi.nlm.nih.gov/pubmed/12814717
	Also HIV, RSV, and herpes viruses	https://www.ncbi.nlm.nih.gov/pubmed/27815461
		https://www.ncbi.nlm.nih.gov/pubmed/23643542
	The antiviral and antimicrobial activities of licorice	https://www.ncbi.nlm.nih.gov/pmc/articles/PMC4629407/
Myricetin (found in tomatoes, oranges, nuts, berries, tea, and red wine	Potently inhibits the SARS-CoV coronavirus helicase protein in vitro. Myricetin is structurally similar to fisetin, luteolin, and quercetin.	https://www.ncbi.nlm.nih.gov/pubmed/22578462
Olive Leaf	Significant antiviral activity against *respiratory syncytial virus* and *para-influenza type 3 virus* Also antiviral activities against: herpes mononucleosis, hepatitis virus, rotavirus, bovine rhinovirus, canine parvovirus, and feline leukemia virus	https://www.ncbi.nlm.nih.gov/pmc/articles/PMC3002804/
Oregano (and other compounds)	*Respiratory syncytial virus (RSV), which causes respiratory infections*	Antiviral activity of oregano essential oil and its main compound carvacrol against human and animal viruses. https://www.ncbi.nlm.nih.gov/pubmed/24031796 https://www.ncbi.nlm.nih.gov/pmc/articles/PMC3768712/
	Inhibited 70% of the virus infection.	Antiviral Properties of Supercritical CO2 Extracts from Oregano and Sage

	Carvacrol, thymol, borneol, camphor	https://www.tandfonline.com/doi/full/10.1080/10942912.2012.700539
	Murine norovirus (MNV) stomach flu, herpes simplex virus type-1 (HSV-1) and rotavirus	This study provides novel findings on the antiviral properties of oregano oil and carvacrol against MNV and demonstrates the potential of carvacrol as a natural food and surface sanitizer to control human norovirus. https://www.ncbi.nlm.nih.gov/pubmed/24779581
	Carvacrol (oregano), thymol	These results indicate that compounds affected HSV-1 mostly before adsorption and might interact with the viral envelope. Thymol exhibited a high selectivity index and seems to be a promising candidate for topical therapeutic application as antiviral agent for treatment of herpetic infections. https://www.ncbi.nlm.nih.gov/pubmed/28886313
Peppermint	*respiratory syncytial virus* (RSV)	Aqueous extracts from peppermint, sage, and lemon balm leaves display potent anti-HIV-1 activity by increasing the virion density. https://www.ncbi.nlm.nih.gov/pmc/articles/PMC2288616/
	Antiviral and can decrease levels of inflammatory compounds.	https://www.ncbi.nlm.nih.gov/pmc/articles/PMC6049716/
	A review of the bioactivity and potential health benefits of peppermint tea meant to naturally treat viral infections.	https://www.ncbi.nlm.nih.gov/pubmed/16767798
Resurrection lily (Lycoris radiata), aka red magic lily and other names Active Ingredient: Lycorine	***_Potent antiviral activities against SARS-CoV coronavirus._**	https://www.ncbi.nlm.nih.gov/pubmed/15885816
Rosemary	*influenza*	Animal and test-tube studies using concentrated extracts
	herpes, HIV, and hepatitis A	https://www.ncbi.nlm.nih.gov/pmc/articles/PMC6225463/
	Anti-inflammatory, antioxidant, antimicrobial, antiproliferative, antitumor, and protective, inhibitory and attenuating activities.	https://www.ncbi.nlm.nih.gov/pmc/articles/PMC6325740/ https://www.ncbi.nlm.nih.gov/pubmed/30684236 https://www.ncbi.nlm.nih.gov/

		pubmed/17091431
Saikosaponins (Chinese herbal studies)	***Saikosaponin B2 **significantly inhibited human coronavirus 229E infection** ... pre-infection, coinfection, and post-infection. Furthermore, saikosaponin B2 also showed an inhibitory effect on viral attachment and penetration. The present results indicate that **saikosaponin B2 has potent anticoronaviral activity** and that its mode of action possibly involves interference in the early stage of viral replication, such as absorption and penetration of the virus.	https://www.ncbi.nlm.nih.gov/pubmed/16789928
Sage	HIV-1, prevented the virus from entering cells	Aqueous extracts from peppermint, sage, and lemon balm leaves display potent anti-HIV-1 activity by increasing the virion density. https://www.ncbi.nlm.nih.gov/pmc/articles/PMC2288616/
	HSV-1 and Indiana vesiculovirus	
	Inhibited 70% of the virus infection. Carvacrol, thymol, borneol, camphor	Antiviral Properties of Supercritical CO2 Extracts from Oregano and Sage https://www.tandfonline.com/doi/full/10.1080/10942912.2012.700539
	Antiviral effect at the intracellular level: when added 5 hours before VSV (vesicular stomatitis virus) infection, it caused 100% reduction of CPE (cytopathic effect).	http://agris.fao.org/agris-search/search.do?recordID=RS2009001364
Scutellaria lateriflora (blue skullcap)	Like Myricetin, it potently inhibits the SARS-CoV coronavirus helicase protein in vitro.	https://www.ncbi.nlm.nih.gov/pubmed/22578462
Torreya nucifera (Japanese nutmeg-yew)	Potent inhibitory effect against SARS-CoV coronavirus.	https://www.ncbi.nlm.nih.gov/pubmed/20934345

If you decide to use herbal teas, extracts, infusions, tinctures, essential oils, recipes, or other herbal products, consult your healthcare provider to find out safe usage. Dr. Josh Axe has this to say:

Side Effects
If you use infusions or essential oils, remember that the products are extremely potent and should not be taken for a long period of time. If you use these natural remedies for their antiviral properties, do not consume them for more than two weeks. Giving yourself a break between long doses is important.

If you are pregnant, be cautious of using essential oils and reach out to your health care provider before doing so.

Some of these antiviral herbs interact with medications, so read up on an herb before you begin consuming its extract or essential oil.

> https://draxe.com/nutrition/antiviral-herbs/

If you want to do your own research, a very detailed research paper on **Antiviral Natural Products and Herbal Medicines**, is here -

> https://www.ncbi.nlm.nih.gov/pmc/articles/PMC4032839/

CHAPTER 5 NOTES FROM THE NEWS ON THE INTERNET

China has a lot of big cities with millions of people. Several of them are larger than New York City.

The Chinese people work hard, and one result is some very intense air pollution, way more than we're used to in the US.

You can google if Asians are more susceptible to coronavirus than other ethnic groups. There are several articles on the internet that explain the DNA science behind this, such as -

> Chinese Scientists Find Genetic Explanation For Coronavirus Discriminating By Race
>
> https://tiny.iavian.net/y8pj

If that is true, then -

> If you have a large group of people in China with a hereditary susceptibility to coronavirus, which is a respiratory tract infection, and
>
> If those people are living in a heavy air pollution environment, day in and day out,
>
> Then why would it be surprising that they have a lot of cases?

If you look up "most polluted cities in the world", you will find that a great many of them seem to be in China.

> https://en.m.wikipedia.org/wiki/List_of_most-polluted_cities_by_particulate_matter_concentration

There are a lot of cities like that in India also.

But what about Iran?

Sure enough, in the list of top 500 most air polluted cities in the world, there are a surprising number of not only in China and India, but also in Iran and Poland.

Not so much in the US, in fact none, or very few, depending on what source you look at.

You may also find that a handful of industrial cities in Italy are on that list. Yet no one seems to have figured out why coronavirus cases showed up in Italy. Could be the air had some effect on it.

It has been reported that most of the reported fatalities in Italy (and elsewhere) were people who had some other health issue also and were of advanced age.

All people groups of course have resistance to some things and susceptibility to other things. Some people have remarked that haven't been a lot of coronavirus cases in Africa, compared to the large population there.

> Chinese Scientists Find Genetic Explanation For Coronavirus Discriminating By Race
>
> https://tiny.iavian.net/y8pj

Even though there is heavy Chinese travel to Africa, as of today's date, there haven't been a of reported cases there. Although some people have said they think it's because there aren't a lot of test kits available there yet, so maybe there's just no way to detect them. That could change if there's more testing.

In China, the death rate has been reported as zero in children under 10 and very low, 0.2 percent, in healthy adults.

Some hopeful signs in the news -

- Researchers say a certain spectrum of ultraviolet light — called far-UVC — easily kills airborne flu viruses while posing no risk to people. It could offer a new, inexpensive way to eliminate airborne flu viruses in indoor public spaces such as hospitals, doctors' offices, schools, airports and aircraft, said the team from Columbia University Medical Center in New York City.

  https://www.webmd.com/cold-and-flu/news/20180212/can-uv-light-be-used-to-kill-airborne-flu-virus-#1

- 100 year old man beats the Corona Flu:

  https://nypost.com/2020/03/08/100-year-old-chinese-man-recovers-from-coronavirus-the-oldest-patient-to-beat-illness/

- University of Pennsylvania authority and vaccine expert Paul A. Offit believes that the U.S. death rate from coronavirus will turn out to be "a fraction of 1 percent." adding that there has been a "wild overreaction" to the disease largely because it is new. "We're more the victim of fear than the virus," he said.

  https://reason.com/2020/03/06/trump-says-the-covid-19-death-rate-will-be-a-fraction-of-1-percent-is-he-right/

- Why the silent spread of coronavirus might actually be a good sign. The fact that someone was diagnosed without any known interaction with other infected people sounds scarier than it probably is. Asymptomatic transmission has already been reported in China. In the first reported case, the source patient transmitted the infection to others but never became sick herself. If there are a lot of cases with no symptoms in our communities already, and if this turns out to be common, it's a good thing if many may walk around and not notice. It implies that the case fatality rate—the number of deaths divided by the number of infections—of this novel coronavirus is likely to be far, far lower than the reported statistics.

https://slate.com/technology/2020/02/coronavirus-silent-spread-actually-good-sign.html

Public health groups have told people to stay calm and follow the same basic precautions recommended for preventing flu or any other respiratory virus. Wash your hands, cover your coughs and sneezes, clean household surfaces with disinfectant, maintain good personal hygiene standards, and stay at home from work or school if you're sick.

But don't forget Prayer.

And we have decided to use common sense natural remedies, like garlic and gargling salt water.

In the US, flu is big business. There are several expensive chemicals made by drug companies used to treat various types of flu. It seems very heard to find articles on the internet by drug companies giving details on natural remedies to *prevent* getting a virus in the first place. That could be because they think their chemicals are superior to natural remedies.

Yet believe it or not, many pharmaceuticals are based on centuries old naturopathic treatments. Drug companies scour the Amazon rain forests for exotic plants that contain natural substances which can treat illnesses. Then the drug companies extract the active ingredient, and sell it. That's not necessarily bad, since it costs a lot of money to do all that. The point is, it shows that even giant drug companies recognize the enduring value of natural remedies.

With the coronavirus, it resides in the tissues of the throat and that's why it's far more contagious, allowing it to be spread through the air more easily.

Reality check - it's a fact that the common cold may also actually a type of coronavirus. Since many people find that gargling salt water, eating garlic, and other natural remedies help prevent colds, it makes sense to us that they could maybe help prevent or alleviate coronavirus too.

The common cold uses the throat as a staging area just like the coronavirus does. The common cold as everyone knows is very contagious and spreads through the air by coughs and sneezes. So it makes sense to us to try on the coronavirus what we already know works on colds. So far, the common cold can't be 'cured', but it can be often prevented, and be over sooner, using tried and true remedies that have been around for a thousand years.

Our concern is the closing of businesses, schools, and churches.

Closing of businesses hurts the economy.

Closing of schools disrupts families.

Closing of churches hampers Prayer and Healing services.

We believe that there will be Miracle reports of Healing and of Deliverance from plague.

We hope Churches will continue to broadcast messages of healing over every available method and outlet.

CHAPTER 6 A FEW FACTS AND OPINIONS FROM DOCTORS ON THE INTERNET

Here are some other interesting facts and opinions from doctors and other experts about the coronavirus reported from around the internet. A lot of information on the internet contradicts other information, so you be the judge -

- 80% of the people who have been infected by the novel coronavirus, also referred to as COVID-19, "spontaneously recover," meaning they get better without any specific intervention

- Turns out, females worldwide are much less likely to get it. Lots of cases where a man was quarantined, but wife tested negative.

- The coronavirus is large with a cell diameter of 400-500 microns. Thus, wearing a mask is an effective preventive measure. It will easily be able to keep the virus out.

- The coronavirus does not remain suspended in air that long, except in enclosed spaces. Rather it often falls to the ground. Therefore, some say there is less need to worry about "aerial transmission" or the virus remaining in the air for a long time.

But the farther away you are from someone who is sneezing, the better.

- If it falls on any metal surface, it remains there for about twelve hours. This makes washing of hands very, very important. And washing with soap and water is enough.
- If it falls on fabric, it survives for about nine hours. But washing your clothes or getting out in the sun can be enough to kill the coronavirus.
- The coronavirus can survive on your hands for only ten minutes. But if you use an alcohol-based hand sanitizer, it will kill the germs.
- The coronavirus cannot survive exposure to temperature of 80° F and above. It cannot survive hot climate.
- If you drink hot water and expose yourself to the sun, it will help kill the virus.
- Avoid eating ice cream and other cold food.
- Gargle with warm salt water. This will kill the germs present in your tonsils and prevent it from migrating to your lungs. (Like your Mom told you).
- Medics during the 1918 influenza pandemic found that severely ill flu patients nursed outdoors recovered better than those treated indoors. A combination of fresh air and sunlight seems to have prevented deaths among patients; and infections among medical staff. There is scientific support for this. Research shows that outdoor air is a natural disinfectant. Fresh air can kill the flu virus and other harmful germs. Equally, sunlight is germicidal and there is now evidence it can kill the flu virus.

Here are some statements seen on the internet from various medical experts, again, you be the judge:

"Dr. Drew: I don't claim to know what's motivating the media but, my God, their reporting is absolutely reprehensible. They should be ashamed of themselves. They are creating a panic that is far worse than the viral outbreak. The bottom line, everybody, is listen to Dr. Anthony Fauci of the CDC, do what he tells you, and go about your business. That's the story.
There's not one doctor I've spoken to that disagrees with me. Not one. I ran into an agreement with Dr. Oz last night. He was saying the same thing. We're all telling you the same thing: Stop listening to journalists. They don't know what they're talking about. Listen to the CDC, listen to Anthony Fauci, and do not listen to anybody else. This is the job of those people. They're highly trained professionals. They know what they're doing. Just follow their directions."

"The Pentagon's most secretive military research department is developing a therapeutic "shield" that could provide a new way to boost American's immunity to coronavirus. If scientists are successful, they believe they could create a new therapy with a "manufacturing timeline" in a little over three months."

"So far this flu season, between October 1st and February 15th, the CDC estimates there have been between 29 and 41 million cases of the flu in the U.S., causing between 16,000 and 41,000 deaths. We have nowhere the number of cases or deaths from coronavirus that we see from the flu. There are people walking around out there with the virus that don't even know they have it, it's so mild. So it's going to be much more widespread than we knew. It's going to be much milder than we knew. The 1.7% fatality rate is going to fall."

"The city-state of Singapore ended up subsidizing masks so that every family could have them after people decided to hoard them like they were bottled water in a storm. Pharmacies reported massive shortages of both the masks and sanitizer. Singapore had, as of when the masks were subsidized, 89 confirmed coronavirus cases, and yet panic had caused them to sell out of masks all over the city-state. That means 0.002 percent of the population was infected. Two one-hundredths of the population was infected. In other words, Spanish Influenza this isn't."

"We're dealing with the common cold right now, and we all need to try to avoid a panic and keep things in perspective. Some of the numbers seem to show coronavirus appears far less deadly than the flu."

"Catching it is not *that* easy (if we are careful) and we can kill it quite easily (provided we try). Frequent, careful hand washing, as we now all know, is the most effective way to stop the virus being transmitted, while a solution of ethanol, a solution of hydrogen peroxide or a solution of bleach will disinfect surfaces."

"To be considered at high risk of catching the coronavirus you need to live with, or have direct physical contact with, someone infected, be coughed or sneezed on by them (or pick up a used tissue), or be in face-to-face contact, within [about 6 feet], for more than 15 minutes. We're not talking about passing someone in the street."

"With coronavirus the instructions to avoid it are virtually identical to actions that should be taken to avoid the flu."

"There is no indication that this will last longer than any other virus issue [generally a few months]."

More comments from rigorous and respected medical professionals:

"Your risk of contracting #coronavirus in the U.S. is still low. While it may be spreading, there are likely still a small number of cases. This could change, but it is likely the case right now."

"The 2017-2018 influenza was 60x worse than these corona numbers. It won't be long until corona virus will be history."

"The very first patient in the United States to be diagnosed with the new coronavirus was a man in Snohomish, Washington, who has "fully recovered", county health officials said. The man is now free to leave home isolation and go about regular activities, a spokesperson with the Snohomish County Health District said. The man apparently had contracted the virus after traveling to Wuhan, China in January."

"Israeli scientists are believed to be on the brink of developing the first vaccine against the novel coronavirus, according to Science and Technology Minister Ofir Akunis. If all goes as planned, the vaccine could be ready within a few weeks, according to a release."

"Beyond the epicenter of Wuhan, China — and especially in advanced countries — the fatality rate is much lower, and for most people who are infected, they'll experience a fairly mild illness. For the majority it will likely be a relatively mild illness."

"Emerging research is showing that most of those infected have mild symptoms, and recovering coronavirus victims are now doing just fine all around the world."

"Prototype vaccines exist, treatments are in test mode, and medical journals are filled with research that will point one researcher towards a vaccine."

CHAPTER 7 THE 7 FOLD HEALING MINISTRY OF THE WOMAN

Woman has healing power on this earth, in many areas.

Yet in the US, many woman are working in an office somewhere, or at a store somewhere, using their energy to get a few dollars, while their families are not being blessed by their healing ministry.

In the bible you don't see women having to work. You see the Man providing for the Woman so she doesn't have to work.

In our opinion it is more noble for a woman to heal than to do work for money. We realize this is not a commonly held view in the U.S. But we believe that in general Man Provides and Woman Heals. That's not to say that women can't work, that's up to them. Men sometimes do more of the healing part of family life, nothing wrong with that. We have just found for ourselves that we feel more comfortable with the Man doing the economic work and the Woman doing the home and healing work. We feel that both realms are hard work and the burdens of each are about the same, so it's an equal arrangement. We also feel that when a woman has to work outside the home then come home and take care of that too, it's an unfair burden. That's just our opinion.

If you're a believer in the Jewish Messiah, or even if you're not, you can rejoice in the healing ministry of your wife, your mother, your daughter, your sister, and all the Daughters of Eve.

Proverbs 31 describes A Noble Woman, a Righteous Woman. Someone a successful and good Man wants to marry.

> Many daughters have done noble things,
> but you surpass them all.
>
> A woman who fears the LORD is to be praised.
>
> Let her works praise her at the gates.
>
> She appraises a field and buys it;
> from her earnings she plants a vineyard.
>
> She works hard.
>
> Her husband is known at the city gate,
> where he sits among the elders of the land.
>
> Proverbs 31 BSB

Clara Barton founded the Red Cross. Mother Teresa pioneered health care in India. Marie Curie discovered radium and the x-ray.

Every day, Women minister Healing to their families in 7 key areas -

Healing and Prevention of Disease By Food Wisdom

> Proverbs 31 BSB
>
> A good Woman brings her Man good and not harm all the days of her life.
>
> She is like the merchant ships, bringing her food from afar.
>
> She rises while it is still night to provide food for her household, and meals for her maidservants.

Every day in every country of the world women prepare food which either brings health, or takes it away.

Food is a constant input every day. It is building you up every day - or taking away health one bite at at time.

The Woman is often the gatekeeper of the food that enters your body, which which either builds you up, or takes away your optimal performance, strength, comfort, and longevity.

This viewpoint seems so obvious to us, but it seems so forgotten among churches in America. They have the bible to guide them, so they of all people should realize that God created Woman for many purposes of blessing, and that one of the most important roles any human being can have is the daily ministering of health and healing.

In fact, Women who minister healing to their families, can eliminate 75% of all hospital visits.

Maybe that sounds like a lot but this is because we've read somewhere that it has been estimated that 75% of all hospital admissions have something to do with the digestive tract, whether short term or long term.

That would mean that food is responsible for 75% of all hospital visits and stays.

It could be the short term effects of some food - or illnesses which take years to develop, and which are due to the wrong foods being eaten day in and day out, until finally the body cannot take it anymore.

We believe that God has given women a ministry of healing for themselves and their families. When a woman selects healthy food, free from contaminants as much as it can be these days, she is reducing the chances of illness, and is lengthening the lives of her family.

This is a supremely important and essential task for families, nations, and the human race.

It's a shame that so many women have been pushed into abandoning their families for a few dollars an hour of exhausting work all day. This has certainly contributed to the health care crisis in the US.

All the good work of all the hospitals and all the doctors, cannot replace or overcome the gaping need for women to practice their healing ministry every day through food, care, comfort, and the healing effect of a home made by a woman. There is no replacement for that.

In the produce aisle, my wife expertly selects the freshest, most organic, fruits and vegetables full of nutrients and healing compounds, then turns them into the most delicious meals I've ever tasted. We live in a "food destination". With no disrespect to the many world famous restaurants here, she equals and usually exceeds the top restaurants in this town. In quality, taste, and overall health effects of the food she prepares.

She makes healthy taste good. Really good.

In this book, she shares some of her secrets for food that we use to help make us feel better, look better, and live longer.

Healthy food is not cheap. So I work hard every day to give her the means to get what we need to operate at peak health, energy, stamina, and immune resistance.

I have made it my goal to give my wife the gift of not having to work, so she can perform the miracles of healing that take place when the right foods are chosen, and deliciously prepared.

Healing by food takes place day by day, but it lasts a lifetime.

I have heard preachers talk about praying and "emptying out the hospitals". Well, 75% might be emptied out just by having women giving their families the benefit of the healing gifts that God has given them.

When a woman doesn't cook, relying on frozen dinners, or selects unhealthy or contaminated food out of ignorance or neglect, she and her family suffer.

Ikaria, Where Living to 100 is Commonplace

Reports have found some of the longest living people in the world reside on the Greek Island of Ikaria.

> https://greekcitytimes.com/2019/04/06/ikaria-the-island-where-people-live-longer-than-just-about-anywhere-else-in-the-world/?amp

> https://www.nytimes.com/2012/10/28/magazine/the-island-where-people-forget-to-die.html

The women on Ikaria prepare a unique diet.

Do you suppose there's a connection with all those people who regularly live to be 100, and the meals their women prepare?

Since it is obvious that eating that way makes a huge difference over the "average American diet", you would think that all women believers in the US would be looking at that diet.

Yet many believers have never heard of Ikaria, nor how long they live. It appears from news reports that many if not most Ikarians believe in God.

Maybe God picked them to show the rest of the world how to eat.

Even Jesus foretold the best foods to stay healthy. Modern science once again has validated and confirmed His Word.

Ikarians eat a lot of fish. Jesus used fish to feed the 5,000.

The first meal Jesus cooked after He rose from the dead was fish He made for His disciples.

Was God Himself showing us how to eat in order to live a long time?

We believe God has ordained women with a special ministry of healing, and we wrote this book in part to start proclaiming this message.

Cleanliness

> Proverbs 31 BSB
>
> She watches over the affairs of her household and does not eat the bread of idleness.

Let's face it, germs have a tough time when things are clean. Guys are not known for obsessing about soap.

But every physician will tell you that one of the biggest breakthroughs in medicine in the past 200 years was learning about microbes and how to clean and disinfect, thus killing the invisible germs which cause much of the world's disease.

From the cleaning of food, to the cleaning of household surfaces, Woman stands guard against germs that can't be seen. She thus prevents more diseases than could be counted, since until we get to Heaven, we won't know how many times we escaped illnesses that Woman stopped before they could ever get started.

Comfort Home Quiet Peace Haven Rest Renewal

> Proverbs 31 BSB
>
> When it snows, she has no fear for her household,
> for they are all clothed in scarlet.
> She makes coverings for her bed.

Most people instinctively know that your living space has everything to do with how well rested you are, and how fast you can rebound from stress.

Americans are one of the most sleep deprived nations on earth. We've seen numerous research studies that lack of sleep is a killer. Not enough good sleep literally causes and promotes disease. And it makes your life miserable like you're walking through fog all day.

Women have an innate ability to help their families refresh and rejuvenate. Women create spaces where rest and good sleep can happen. Comfy clean bedding does so much to make us feel happy and well cared for.

The people of Ikaria (see above) know about getting enough rest and exercise.

Strength, Honor, Support, Trust

> Proverbs 31 BSB
>
> Strength and honor are her clothing.

Women nurture their families. As they say, there's nothing "like a woman's touch" to make everything feel alright.

Men just can't do this the way a woman can. We wish that men would not demand that their wives work for a few dollars, and give up the Woman's presence in the home, where she is not just needed, but she is essential.

Wisdom

> Proverbs 31 BSB
>
> She opens her mouth with wisdom,
> and faithful instruction is on her tongue.

I know in our marriage, my wife has so much wisdom in so many things that I marvel and appreciate the amazing Being she is, who

God made to bless me and so many other people.

Why did God make women anyway? If it was to work all day at a job, it would say so in the bible. Yet even the Proverbs 31 woman doesn't have to work. She is cared for by her husband who is known in the gates, and she provides blessing after blessing for her household. (See our Book *Marriage of Fire* for an extensive study of this).

We would like to see the proper, and noble, roles of Men and Women restored as God created us to be.

Noble Friendship

> Proverbs 31 BSB
>
> Noble character in a Woman is far more precious than rubies.

A US President once said that if you live in Washington DC, and need a friend - get a dog.

Mothers, fathers, wives, husbands, children - all need the friendship of their mothers, daughters, sisters, and wives.

This is a special, and holy, relationship that partakes of the nature of God Himself.

God called Abraham His friend. That means that friendship comes directly from God.

Women, your family needs your friendship, which brings blessing that can't be found anywhere else, and which can never be erased.

Beauty Clothes and Fashion

> Proverbs 31 BSB
>
> She selects wool and flax
> and works with eager hands.

> Her clothing is fine linen and purple.
> She makes linen garments and sells them.
> She delivers sashes to the merchants.

If beauty were bad, why did God create it? We need to live in homes where there is beauty, art, and fine decorations which the Woman of the House has searched out and placed to bring enjoyment to her family.

Do you remember as a child when you visited your friend's houses? Did you notice that they weren't as "homey" as the house your mother had made?

When you visit the home of a noble woman, don't you notice how comfortable, rested, refreshed, inspired, and uplifted it makes you feel?

Only a Woman can do that.

Women create a safe haven where their family can rest and be restored day after day.

CHAPTER 8 SECRETS OF NOBLE WOMEN ABOUT HEALING AND PREVENTION OF DISEASE

These are some secrets that my wife uses for our home, which come from her upbringing, trial and error, reading various research studies, and general articles on the internet. They are not recommendations for anyone else, just offered as information about what we do.

PROPER DIET

Eating in a healthy manner is like a treasure chest lost in the modern century.

The poorest people called peasants of the dark ages in Europe ate better than a lot of today's wealthy and semi-wealthy people.

Their regular diet consisted of salmon and bread.

Jesus fed the 5,000 with two fish and five loaves of bread (Matthew 14:13-21).

The Greek Ikarian diet has lots of fish and vegetables, and remains one of the top healthiest diets in the world.

People consuming it tend to -

> Look and feel younger than their actual age

> Live longer

> Have clear minds

We would like to experience those three things every day.

God created these foods so we can have these things.

Remember the Hebrew princes of Daniel? Daniel's men ate vegetables.

> <u>Daniel 1</u> 11 Daniel then said to the guard whom the chief official had appointed over Daniel, Hananiah, Mishael, and Azariah, 12 "Please test your servants for ten days: **Give us nothing but vegetables to eat and water to drink.** 13 Then compare our appearance with that of the young men who eat the royal food, and treat your servants in accordance with what you see." 14 So he agreed to this and tested them for ten days.
>
> 15 **At the end of the ten days they looked healthier and better nourished than any of the young men who ate the royal food.** 16 So the guard took away their choice food and the wine they were to drink and gave them vegetables instead.
>
> 17 To these four young men God gave knowledge and understanding of all kinds of literature and learning. And Daniel could understand visions and dreams of all kinds.

Fish and veggies is in the Jewish Bible.

It's on Ikaria.

Fish and veggies clearly works.

Mediterranean countries are from the coast of Portugal, all the way down to the island of Cyprus. Some might say, well it's in their genes - and that may be partially true, but we think anybody can profit from a Mediterranean diet.

One of the components of this diet is lettuce. The problem is that we have found only one way of properly cleaning green lettuce and when it's not done properly and eaten, it often causes stomach problems like diarrhea.

Because of its leaves, just like kale, it tends to store bacteria that should not be ingested.

To make sure that our lettuce is ready to be consumed, first we will find a deep bowl, then cut the leaves of the lettuce in half (any obvious withered leaves and filth are to be removed).

Then we will place those leaves in the bowl as we are cutting them and fill the bowl with cold water to the top.

Then we place a plate on top of the bowl to make sure no dirt falls into the bowl. Leave the lettuce in there for at least 30 minutes, but usually we might want to leave it for an hour or two. This helps purify the lettuce leaves from filth that is invisible to the human eye.

After an hour or two, take a strainer and rinse the leaves again with cold water. It is now ready to be consumed or stored in the fridge. In this way, it will help make a barrier to stomach bugs and diarrhea from eating home prepared lettuce.

You have probably seen news stories about outbreaks of diarrhea from lettuce in various restaurant chains, including fast food. It doesn't necessarily mean the lettuce was bad, it might mean that it wasn't cleaned properly. We've experienced this ourselves while traveling, so my wife inspects any lettuce we might eat in a restaurant. In fact, we have a list of foods that seem to be generally safe in restaurants, and we try to stick to those when we have lunch and dinner meetings, etc.

What are some other foods you could incorporate in your diet if you want to eat Mediterranean like we do?

(you can print these on a list and use it as your food shopping list)

Some Foods Eaten by People in the Mediterranean

Food	Comments
VEGGIES	
	These veggies are generally safer to eat if someone has histamine issues or overly sensitive stomach, though be careful with spinach:
	Lettuce
	Just like lettuce all these require to be cleansed really well: Broccoli Cauliflower Chard Green onion
	Garlic
	Beets
	Ginger
	Onion
	Green beans
	Zucchini
	Carrots
	Cabbage
	Bell peppers
	Radish
	Celery

	Lima beans
	Black eyes peas
	Spinach
	Can be consumed by people with no food sensitivity:
	Tomatoes
	We like Ginger Garlic Fried Rice as a nice side dish
FRUIT	
	Lemon
	Bananas
	Apples
	Oranges
	Watermelon
	Mango
	Pomegranate
	Apricot
	Peach
	Melon
	Pear

	Plantains
	(Mostly safe to consume by anyone, and much better if organic)
BERRIES	
	Raspberries
	Blackberries
	Blueberries
	Cherries
	Grapes
	Strawberries
	(If you have food sensitivity, you probably should avoid strawberries)
OLIVES	
	We use olives to put on our salad or homemade pizza dishes, and we add anchovies because we like them. We can also add tomatoes to our salads (only for my husband because he is not allergic to them), croutons, some olive oil, or anything else we might like. We make sure we completely discard canola oil from our diet, as there is research that says it is not natural and not safe to consume. We use fresh olive oil instead.

SHELTER FROM THE PLAGUE

FISH	
	Salmon, halibut, mackerel, or any other type of fish with less mercury (do your own research on this)
	Sushi
	Smoked salmon
	Shrimp
	Canned tuna in water, we have read that skipjack especially has less mercury in it
MEAT	
	Grass-fed red meat, particularly lamb
	(My wife introduced me to lamburgers, and they are my favorite now)
	Chicken
	We meat in moderation - but we don't eat trans fat, processed sausages, and such. According to Ikarians you can eat as much meat as it feels good to you though, some barely eat meat and feel good, and some need meat to feel good and have energy. Even my husband gets tired of it sometimes and wants only Greek salad for the rest of the week.

MILK AND YOGURT	
	A-2 Cow or goat's milk
	Some women try consuming milk if they have contractions before their period, it contains calcium and it may help ease pains.
	Butter (grass fed is considered better)
	Eggs
	If you have a problem digesting chicken eggs, aka you have pains in your tummy, diarrhea, or nausea, you can try replacing them like we did with duck eggs because they are easier for us to digest and seem to cause fewer stomach problems.
	Yogurt and probiotic drinks
	Yogurt has healthy bacteria in it and helps us in our digestion and we can consume it if we feel "stuffed" or if we just naturally like eating yogurt. Probiotic drinks are similar but can be replaced with probiotic supplements.
	Mozzarella
	We pick cheese based on our sensitivity level, if you have food sensitivity you can try mozzarella or provolone

	cheese or American cheese or cottage cheese. If you have no food sensitivity, you can often try whichever cheese you like.
	Cottage cheese
	Cream cheese
	Sour cream
	Also do not consume too much sugar, but if we women feel we need chocolate from time to time, there is some research that says it has minerals that women's bodies need.
COOKING SPICES	
	Rosemary
	Oregano
	Parsley
	Tarragon
	Ground turmeric
	Ground raw garlic
	Thyme
DRINKS	

	Green tea
	Fresh pressed fruit juices
	Herbal teas
	Grape juice
	We drink any drink that is not from concentrate, any fruit juices we might like, and herbal teas. Green tea is a powerful antioxidant, it can clear out our skin and acne and aids in digestion.
OTHER	
	Black, red, brown rice
	Croissants
	Plain potato chips (once in a while)
	Nuts
	Honey (raw is better)
	Oats
	Pasta
	Corn grits
	Bread
	(whole wheat bread and we don't eat it too often)

The above just gives you a general idea of what our experience is like to eat like the Ikarians, but you can add or leave out things as you please if you want to try that idea.

Do your own research and find out what works for you. The above works for us, but others might need to modify for various reasons.

OLIVE OIL

Olive oil has been used for beauty and cooking for thousands of years. The Bible talks about putting olive oil on the wounds of captives as a sign of mercy and healing (2 Chronicles 28.15).

Women have been using olive oil for many different purposes, to soften the skin of face or heels or rough skin areas, to remove makeup, to use it in addition to other oils for making a perfume body oil, to heal skin scars.

It has anti-inflammatory and anti-aging properties. The Bible talks about "cakes" made with olive oil as an offering (Exodus 29:2), anointing one's head with oil (Psalm 23:5), and eating fine flour, honey, and oil (Ezekiel 16:13). That last one is a "healthy pastry".

We, from all Nations including the Jews, have all been grafted into the olive tree of Israel by being born again (Romans 11:17), so it is clear that Bible has a lot to say about olives and its oil and its tree and roots.

What does science say are the benefits of consuming olive oil?

- Full of fatty acids reducing inflammation
- Lowers the risk of heart disease
- Contains vitamins E and K
- Full of antioxidants (antioxidants are substances protecting

your body from toxins in the environment as well as biological toxins such as cancer, heart problems, etc.)
- Lowers the risk of stroke
- It does not cause you to gain weight, it may even help you to lose weight if consuming it regularly
- Reduces risk of type 2 diabetes
- Fights bacteria in stomach known to cause stomach ulcers and stomach cancer

It is just the healthiest oil on the planet. Made by God for us.

"And the dove came back to him in the evening, and behold, in her mouth was a freshly plucked olive leaf. So Noah knew that the waters had subsided from the earth." (Genesis 8:11)

Some people also make a healthy tea with freshly brewed olive leaves, it is an important ingredient in the Mediterranean diet.

CHAPTER 9 MORE SECRETS OF NOBLE WOMEN

HEALING

Churches are full of believers wanting, needing, and being desperate for healing. But a lot of those issues might be eliminated with researching what food is good and what is safe for you to consume, which we have already covered in the chapter before. Here we will talk about other common issues that plague men and women and how we personally help our bodies to heal naturally.

COLD (ALSO VIRUS, PAINFUL THROAT)

If someone happens to get a cold, there are a few things we've found we can do that may help us get back on our feet pretty quick.

There are several things we will need:

Tea for hurting throat or if we don't have it, we may use ginger or chamomile tea; add honey and quarter of a lemon juice to it; consume this at least 3 times a day.

We can use these supplements —

- vitamin C
- slippery elm

- echinacea
- garlic and/or allicin extract

Slippery elm and tea can help soothe a hurting throat and help us blow through our nose and cough out all the junk from the germs.

Vitamin C and echinacea may help strengthen our immune system, together with allicin extract which is the active part of garlic that kills the germs and viruses and bacteria.

Also when we notice colder weather, place a scarf around our throat and don't leave it exposed to harsh weather.

PAINFUL PMS
(This symptom can be a sign of other problems, so talk to your doctor)

If a woman happens to have painful periods, she may have blood clots that she passes as she pees. To make sure she doesn't suffer for days on end, two or three days before your period is due, some women have tried blood thinning supplements as natto-serra and ginkgo. A few pills of each one once a day before a period may be enough. This may help ensure blood flow is uninterrupted. Again, if you think of trying this, be sure to ask your doctor.

We could also use Iron supplement, Inositol, Vitamin D, and Folic Acid. This sometimes aids in hormonal balance in women.

If a woman keeps having painful contractions before or during her menstruation, she could maybe try both Magnesium and Calcium supplements together. Magnesium helps calcium release all its properties, as opposed to only consuming a calcium supplement. This may help make contractions cease, but ask your doctor.

SENSITIVE OR OVERLY-SENSITIVE SKIN

If a woman has problems with skin sensitivity, it is very important what she eats and drinks. It may help to consume tea and water often.

Dealing with sensitive skin is very hard as skin is the largest organ and often skin irritations make someone overly moody or extra sensitive, but there can be things to do to ease every day life.

Using only skin friendly soaps - charcoal soap, oatmeal soap, Dead Sea mud soap, for example. Using skin sensitive hand creams as well - soothing lotions for sensitive skin or oils that will help the skin heal naturally.

For the face, using only safe soaps, skin cleansers, or serums. Some women use micellar water which doesn't contain mineral oil as this can irritate sensitive skin more Some women also use vitamin C or hyaluronic acid serum. As a face mask, Dead Sea mud but never masks which contain alcohol or substances which you cannot pronounce.

For body washing, use a very mild cleaning agent, never scented or with fragrances.

FOOD POISONING

If we happened to have caught a stomach bug (which sometimes happens in restaurants or dining places) and now feel weak, have fever, feel nausea, and/or are vomiting, have constant diarrhea and an upset tummy, we need to rest our stomach and take it easy on our physical activities.

We should rest as much as we possibly can and eat bland foods, and drink water or broth.

Foods we have tried which helped us are:

- bananas
- crackers
- toast
- applesauce

- plain rice
- plain sliced turkey
- plain potatoes

ACNE

If someone has hormonal acne, they might research supplements which aid in hormonal balance. Hormonal acne is acne which appears during or before a period.

To deal with acne, some women use a face humidifier. They are fairly cheap and a good investment. Using a face humidifier can help open pores and cleanse skin impurities.

Use either mild soap or mild micellar water to clean the face everyday. After that, use rose water toner, it is mild and natural and can even the skin out. We don't have to waste our money for overly priced fake rose water cleaners, we can get the real thing for much cheaper at a grocery store or mediterranean market because it is used for cooking.

Then we can try a facial mist toner because this makes our skin glow and gives it moisture. After this top it off with a facial serum.

DIARRHEA

If we are having issues with diarrhea, or it just happened to come at a really odd time when we really don't need it, it would be best to stay hydrated. Drink plenty of water. We can also use charcoal pills, eat apples, and drink probiotic drinks to help aid in creating healthy bacteria.

INDIGESTION

If we feel indigestion because we ate a lot of meat, we might cut beef and pork out of our menu and replace it with lamb.

Foods which can help cleanse us from the inside out if we're having indigestion are:

- green lettuce
- yogurt
- blueberries
- kefir
- oats
- lemon water

We usually use probiotic pills before every meal.

ALLERGY

If we have issues breathing properly or are getting hives or skin irritations, besides eating safe foods, we can consider several supplements which can help keep our health at the top:

- Histamine block pills
- Quercetin with bromelain
- Supplements for a healthy liver and kidneys

CHAPTER 10 HEALING AND PROTECTION AGAINST DISEASE IN THE END TIMES

Paul said that all Christians have been brought into Israel. (See our book *One New People*). If you believe this, then embrace and receive your Israelite heritage and claim verses of Healing and Protection from plague.

> The Israelites in Goshen were kept from the plagues by the blood of the lamb
>
> Daniel in the Lions den
>
> The three Hebrew children in the furnace of fire

Even in Exodus, God foretold that all Nations would be like natives of the land and come into Israel -

> Exodus 12.47 The whole congregation of Israel must celebrate it. 48 If a foreigner resides with you and wants to celebrate the LORD's Passover, all the males in the household must be circumcised; then he may come near to celebrate it, and *he shall be like a native of the land*. But no uncircumcised man may eat of it. 49 *The same law shall apply to both the native and the foreigner who resides among you.*" BSB

So if you have accepted Jesus the Jewish Messiah, all these promises *belong to you!*

We believe these Healing, Protection, and Deliverance Scriptures will encourage you and build your faith for healing, deliverance, and divine protection. "Faith comes by reading/hearing the Word of God."

Whenever you see fear based headlines, open this book and read what God has to say about it. The Lord lifts up a banner against all our enemies.

If you ever need healing, mediate on the healing verses section. They will build your faith to believe God. Read and pray every day for your healing. Jesus the Jewish Messiah still heals today.

Use the space provided near each Scripture to write down -

- Answers to prayer you have received

- Insights you have received from God

- Misc notes you want to remember

While you're reading these Healing and Protection Scriptures, call on the Lord for these promises to happen in your life. He will do what He promised for any person who calls on Him. It doesn't matter what race or country you are from, or even what you have done in the past.

These promises now belong to all Nations and God will help everyone who calls on the Name of Yeshua (Jesus) the Jewish Messiah.

The Hebrew meaning of the Name Yeshua (Jesus) is "Salvation". He will save all those who call upon Him.

SCRIPTURES FOR THIS TIME IN AMERICA

Reference	Scripture
Matthew 24 BSB	6 You will begin to hear of wars and rumors of wars, but see to it that you are not alarmed. These things must happen, but the end is still to come. 7 Nation will rise against nation, and kingdom against kingdom. *There will be famines and plagues and earthquakes in various places.* 8 All these are the beginning of birth pains.
Exodus 9.6 BSB	*…but not one animal belonging to the Israelites died.*
Exodus 9.26 BSB	*The only place where it did not hail was in the land of Goshen, where the Israelites lived.*
Exodus 10 BSB	22 Total darkness covered all the land of Egypt for three days. 23 No one could see each other, and for three days no one left his place. *Yet all the Israelites had light in their dwellings.*
Exodus 12.13 BSB	When I see the blood, I will pass over you. *No plague will fall on you to destroy you.* [The Israelites in Goshen were kept from the plagues by the blood.]
Exodus 12 BSB	47 The whole congregation of Israel must cele-

	brate it. 48If a foreigner resides with you and wants to celebrate the LORD's Passover, all the males in the household must be circumcised; then he may come near to celebrate it, and *he shall be like a native of the land*. But no uncircumcised man may eat of it. 49*The same law shall apply to both the native and the foreigner who resides among you.*"
Daniel 6 BSB	19At the first light of dawn, the king got up and hurried to the den of lions. 20When he reached the den, he cried out in a voice of anguish, "O Daniel, servant of the living God, has your God, whom you serve continually, been able to deliver you from the lions?" 21Then Daniel replied, "O king, may you live forever! 22*My God sent His angel and shut the mouths of the lions. They have not hurt me*, for I was found innocent in His sight, and I have done no wrong against you, O king." 23The king was overjoyed and gave orders to lift Daniel out of the den, and *when Daniel was lifted out of the den, no wounds whatsoever were found on him, because he had trusted in his God.* 25Then King Darius wrote to the people of every nation and language throughout the land: "May your prosperity abound. 26I hereby decree that in every part of my kingdom, men are to tremble in fear before the God of Daniel: For He is the living God, and He endures forever; His kingdom will never be destroyed, and His dominion will never end. 27*He delivers and rescues*; He performs signs and wonders in the heavens and on the earth, for *He has rescued Daniel from the power of the lions.*" 28So Daniel prospered during the reign of Darius and the reign of Cyrus the Persian.

Daniel 3 BSB	22The king's command was so urgent and the furnace so hot that the fiery flames killed the men who carried up Shadrach, Meshach, and Abednego (Daniel, the name Belteshazzar; to Hananiah, Shadrach; to Mishael, Meshach; and to Azariah, Abednego). 23And these three men, Shadrach, Meshach, and Abednego, fell into the blazing fiery furnace. 24Suddenly King Nebuchadnezzar jumped up in amazement and asked his advisers, "Did we not throw three men, firmly bound, into the fire?" "Certainly, O king," they replied. 25"Look!" he exclaimed. "I see four men, unbound and unharmed, walking around in the fire—and the fourth looks like a son of the gods!" 26Then Nebuchadnezzar approached the door of the blazing fiery furnace and called out, "Shadrach, Meshach, and Abednego, servants of the Most High God, come out!"
	So ***Shadrach, Meshach, and Abednego came out of the fire***, 27and when the satraps, prefects, governors, and royal advisers had gathered around, they saw that ***the fire had no effect on the bodies of these men. Not a hair of their heads was singed, their robes were unaffected, and there was no smell of fire on them.*** 28Nebuchadnezzar declared, ***"Blessed be the God of Shadrach, Meshach, and Abednego, who has sent His angel and delivered His servants who trusted in Him.*** They violated the king's command and risked their lives rather than serve or worship any god except their own God. 29Therefore I decree that the people of any nation or language who say anything offensive against the God of Shadrach, Meshach, and Abednego will be cut into pieces and their houses reduced to rubble. ***For there is no other god who can deliver in this way."***

SHELTER FROM THE PLAGUE

	30 *Then the king promoted Shadrach, Meshach, and Abednego in the province of Babylon.*
1 Kings 8 BSB	37 *When famine or plague comes upon the land, or blight or mildew or locusts or grasshoppers, or when their enemy besieges them in their cities, whatever plague or sickness may come, 38 may whatever prayer or petition Your people Israel make—each knowing his own afflictions and spreading out his hands toward this temple— 39 be heard by You from heaven, Your dwelling place.* And may You forgive and act, and repay each man according to all his ways, since You know his heart—for You alone know the hearts of all men— 40 so that they may fear You all the days they live in the land that You gave to our fathers.
	41 *And as for the foreigner who is not of Your people Israel but has come from a distant land because of Your name— 42 for they will hear of Your great name and mighty hand and outstretched arm —when he comes and prays toward this temple, 43 then may You hear from heaven, Your dwelling place, and do according to all for which the foreigner calls to You. Then all the peoples of the earth will know Your name and fear You, as do Your people Israel, and they will know that this house I have built is called by Your Name.*
Numbers 16 BSB	46 *Go take your golden lamp of fire and place fire from the altar in it, and add incense. Go quickly to the congregation and make atonement for them, because wrath has come out from the LORD; the plague has begun."* 47 So Aaron took the golden fire lamp as Moses had ordered and ran into the midst of the assembly. *And seeing that the plague had begun among the*

> *people, he offered the incense and made atonement for the people. 48He stood between the living and the dead, and the plague was halted.*

HEALING MINISTRY OF JESUS THE MESSIAH

All Scriptures in this section ABPE unless otherwise noted

Reference	Scripture
Acts 10:37-38	You also are aware of the Word that has come to all Judea, which went out from Galilee after the baptism that Yohannan preached, about Yeshua who was from Nazareth, whom God anointed with The Spirit of Holiness and with Power, and he was traveling and *healing those injured by the evil one*, because God was with Him.
Acts 3:6	Shimeon Peter said [to a lame beggar], "I have no gold or silver, but what I do have, I give to you - In the Name of Yeshua The Messiah, the Nazarene, *stand up and walk*."
Acts 4:30-31	"And *stretch your hand for healing and for mighty acts and for signs to occur* in the Name of your Holy Son Yeshua." And when they had prayed and made supplication, the place was shaken in which they were assembled, and they were all filled with The Spirit of Holiness, and they were speaking the word of God openly.
Acts 9:33-34	And he found one man whose name was Annis who was lying in bed and had been paralyzed for eight years. And Shimeon Peter said to him, "Annis, *Yeshua The Messiah is healing you. Stand and make your bed*', *and at that moment he got up.*"
Isaiah 53:5 | YLT	He is pierced for our transgressions, bruised for our iniquities, the chastisement of our peace is on him, and by his wounds *there is healing to us*.

John 9:5-11	"As long as I am in the world, I am The Light of the world." And when he had said these things, he spat on the ground and formed clay from his spittle and he smeared it on the eyes of him who was blind. And he said to him, "Go wash in the baptismal pool of Shilokha", and he went on, he washed, *and as he was coming, he saw.* But his neighbors and those who had seen him begging before were saying: "Was this not he who sat and begged?" Some were saying, "This is he", and some were saying, "No, but he is someone like him", but he said, "I am he." They were saying to him, *"How were your eyes opened?" He answered and said to them, "A man by the name 'Yeshua' made clay and anointed me on my eyes and said to me, 'Go wash in the water of Shilokha', and I went, I washed and I saw."*
Luke 10:8-9	"And whatever city you enter, and they receive you, eat anything that is offered to you." *And heal those who are sick in it and say to them, "The Kingdom of God has come near to you."*
Luke 13:11-13	A woman was there who had a spirit of affliction eighteen years, and she was bent over, and she had not been able to be straightened at all. But Yeshua saw her and he called her and said to her, *"Woman, you are released from your affliction." And he laid his hand upon her and at once she was straightened, and she glorified God.*
Luke 14:1-6	And it was that when he entered the house of one of the leaders of the Pharisees to eat bread on the Sabbath day, and they were observing him, Behold, one man who was swollen with fluid was there before him. And Yeshua answered and said to the Scribes and to the Pharisees, *"Surely it is legal to heal on the Sabbath." But they were silent, and he held him and healed him and he dismissed him. And he said to them, "Who of you, whose child or ox should fall in a pit on the Sabbath day, would not at once pull and lift him out?"* And they could not give him an answer to this.
Luke 17:17-19	And when he approached to enter a certain village, ten men who were lepers met him, and they stood afar off. And they lifted up their voices and they were saying, "Our Rabbi*, Yeshua, have mercy on us!" And when he saw them, he said to them, *"Go show yourselves to the*

	priests", *and as they were going, they were purified.* But one of them, when he saw that he was purified, he returned to him and he was praising God with a loud voice. And he fell on his face before the feet of Yeshua as he gave thanks to him, and this one was a Samaritan. But Yeshua answered and he said, "Were there not ten who were purified? Where are the nine?" "Have they neglected to come give glory to God, except this one who is from a foreign people?" And he said to him, *"Arise; go. Your faith has saved you."*
Luke 4:18	NIV	"The Spirit of THE LORD GOD OF ISRAEL is upon me. He has anointed me to preach the Good News to the poor. *He has sent me to heal the sick, to proclaim liberty to captives, restore sight to the blind, and to bring deliverance to the oppressed".*
Luke 4:41	*He cast out many demons from many people.* As they left, the demons screamed and they were saying, "You are The Messiah, the Son of God!" And He rebuked them and did not allow them to say that they knew that he was The Messiah.
Luke 5:17-25	And it happened on one of the days when Yeshua was teaching, people had come from every village of Galilee, and of Judea, and of Jerusalem, and *the power of THE LORD GOD OF ISRAEL was there to heal them.* And men brought a man on a pallet who was paralyzed, and they were seeking to enter to place him in front of Him. And when they found no way to bring him in because of the crowd of people, they went up by themselves to the roof and lowered him with the pallet from the tiles into the center, in front of Yeshua. *When Yeshua saw their faith, he said to the paralyzed man: "Man, your sins are forgiven you."* And the Scribes and Pharisees began to think, and they were saying, "Who is this who speaks blasphemy? Who is able to forgive sins except God alone?" But Yeshua knew their thoughts; he answered and said to them, "What thoughts are entertained by you in your heart?" *"Which is easier: to say, 'Your sins are forgiven you', or to say, 'Arise and walk?' But that you may know that The Son of Man is authorized in the earth to forgive sins",* he said to the paralyzed man, *"I say to you, arise, pick up your pallet and go to your house."* And at once he arose before their eyes and took

	up his pallet and he went on to his house as he praised God. And astonishment seized everyone and they were praising God, and they were filled with awe and they were saying, *"We have seen wonders today."*
Luke 6:19	All those in the crowds were seeking to touch him, for *power was going out from Him and was healing all of them.*
Luke 8:50,54-55	Yeshua said to the father of the girl, *"Do not be afraid; only have faith, and she will live." Yeshua held her by her hand and he called her, and he said, "Little girl, arise."* And *her spirit returned, and at once she arose, and he commanded them to give her food.*
Mark 1:29-34	They went out from the synagogue and came to the house of Shimeon Peter and Andrewas with Yaqob and Yohannan. And the mother-in-law of Shimeon was lying ill with fever and they told Him about her. *He came near and took her by the hand and raised her up and at once her fever left her and she was waiting on them.* In the evening at the going down of the sun *they brought to him all of them who had been ill and demon possessed.* And the whole city was assembled at the door. *He healed multitudes that had become ill with various diseases and he cast out many evil spirits.* He did not allow them to speak because they knew Who He was.
Mark 10:46-52	When Yeshua went out from Jericho with his disciples and the many crowds, Timai, a blind man, was sitting on the side of the road begging. Then he heard that it was Yeshua the Nazarene, and he began to cry out and to say, "Son of David, have mercy on me!" And many were rebuking him that he would be quiet, but he was crying out all the more and he said, "Son of David, have mercy on me!" Yeshua stood and commanded that they would call him and they called the blind man and they were saying to him, "Take heart, arise, he is calling for you." The blind man threw off his garment and arose, coming to Yeshua. And *Yeshua said to him, "What do you want me to do for you?" But the blind man said to him, "Rabbi*, that I might see." And Yeshua said to him, "See*; your faith has saved you.", and immediately he saw, and he was going down the road.*

SHELTER FROM THE PLAGUE

Mark 5:25-34	But there was a certain woman who had a flow of blood twelve years who had suffered greatly from many physicians and had spent everything that she had and she had not been helped at all, but she had become even worse. When she heard about Yeshua, she came in the press of the crowd from behind him and she touched his garment, for she said, "If I touch even his garment, I shall be saved." *At once the fountain of her blood dried up, and she knew in her body that she was healed of her plague.* But Yeshua knew in himself at once that power had gone out from him and he turned to the crowds and he said, "Who has touched my garment?" And his disciples were saying to him, "You see the crowd pressing against you, and do you say, 'Who has touched me?'" And he was gazing that he might see who had done this. But that woman, being afraid and trembling, for she knew what had happened to her, came and fell down before him and told him all the truth. But he said to her, *"My daughter, your faith has saved you; go in peace and be whole from your disease."*
Mark 6:56	*Wherever he entered a village or city, they were laying the sick in the streets, and they were begging him if they might touch even the fringe of his garment, and all those who were touching it were healed.*
Matthew 10:1,7-8	Yeshua called his twelve disciples and *He gave them authority over foul spirits to cast them out, and to heal every ailment and disease.* "But go especially to the sheep that have been lost of the house of Israel. As you are going, preach and say 'The Kingdom of Heaven has come near.' *Heal the sick, purify the lepers, and cast out demons.* Freely you have received, freely give."
Matthew 4:23-24	Yeshua traveled through all Galilee and he taught in their assemblies and preached the Good News of the Kingdom and *cured every sickness and disease among the people.* His fame was heard in all Syria, and *they brought to him all those who had become ill with various diseases, those who were afflicted with severe pain, and the demon possessed, and lunatics and paralytics, and he healed them all.*

Matthew 8:1-3	When Yeshua came down from the mountain, great crowds followed him. And behold a certain leper came worshiping him, and he said, "My lord, if you are willing, you are able to purify me." *Yeshua, stretched out his hand, touched him, and said, "I am willing. Be purified", and at that moment his leprosy was cured.*
Matthew 8:14-17	Yeshua came to Shimeon Peter's house, and saw his mother-in-law who lay in bed because a fever had seized her. *He touched her hand, and the fever left her.* She arose and she was waiting on him. *When it was evening, they brought many demon possessed before him, and he cast their demons out with a Word, and all those who had become ill, and he healed them.* So that would be fulfilled which was said by Isaiah the Prophet, who said: *"He will take our pains and he will bear our sicknesses."*
Matthew 9:20-22	A woman who had a flow of blood for twelve years, came from behind him and she touched the hem of his garment. *For she was saying in herself, "If only I may touch his clothes, I shall be healed." Yeshua turned, and saw her, and he said to her, "Take heart my daughter, your faith has saved you." And the woman was healed from that moment.*
Matthew 9:27-29	When Yeshua passed by there, two blind men followed him who cried out and they were saying, "Have pity on us, son of David." *When he had come to the house, the blind men came near to him. Yeshua said to them, "Do you believe that I am able to do this?" They said to him, "Yes, Our Lord." Then he touched their eyes, and he said, "Just as you have believed, let it be done to you." And at once their eyes were opened.*
Matthew 9:35	Yeshua traveled through all the cities and all the villages and he was teaching in their assemblies and preaching the Good News of the Kingdom. *He healed all their diseases and all ailments.*
Matthew 9:5-7	*Which is easier, to say, "Your sins are forgiven you", or to say, "Arise and walk?" Now, that you may know that The Son of Man has authority in the earth to forgive sins, I say to this paralytic, "Stand up, take your pallet and go to your house." And he stood up and he went to his house.*

HEALING SCRIPTURES

Reference	Scripture
Deuteronomy 7:15	**The Lord will keep you free from every disease.** He will not inflict on you the horrible diseases you knew in Egypt.
Exodus 23:25	Worship the LORD your God, and **his blessing will be on your food and water. He will take away sickness from among you…**
Isaiah 38:16-17	**You restored me to health and let me live.** Surely it was for my benefit that I suffered such anguish. In your love **you kept me from the pit of destruction**; you have put all my sins behind your back.
Isaiah 53:4-5	**Surely he took up our pain and bore our suffering, yet we considered him punished by God, smitten by him, and afflicted. But he was pierced for our transgressions, he was crushed for our iniquities; the punishment that brought us peace was on him, and by his wounds we are healed.**
Isaiah 57:18-19	I have seen their ways, but **I will heal them**; I will guide them and restore comfort to Israel's mourners, creating praise on their lips. Peace, peace, to those far and near, says the LORD. **And I will heal them.**
Isaiah 58:8	Then your light will break forth like the dawn, and **your healing will quickly appear**; then your righteousness will go before you, and the glory of the LORD will be your rear guard.
James 5:14-15	Is anyone among you sick? Let him call for the elders of the church, and let them pray over him, anointing him with oil in the name of the Lord. And **the prayer**

	of faith will save the one who is sick, and the Lord will raise him up.
James 5:16	Therefore, confess your sins to one another and **pray for one another, that you may be healed.** The effectual fervent prayer of a righteous man availeth much.
James 5:6	Therefore confess your sins to each other and **pray for each other so that you may be healed.** The prayer of a righteous person is powerful and effective.
Jeremiah 17:14	**Heal me, O Lord, and I will be healed**; save me and I will be saved, for you are the one I praise.
Jeremiah 30:17	But **I will restore you to health and heal your wounds**,' declares the LORD
Jeremiah 33:6	Behold, **I will bring health and healing to them. I will heal my people.** I will reveal to them abundance of prosperity and will let them enjoy abundant peace and security.
John 3 1:2	**I pray that you may enjoy good health and that all may go well with you, even as your soul is getting along well.**
Kings 2 20:5	Thus says the Lord, the God of your ancestor David: I have heard your prayer, I have seen your tears; indeed, **I will heal you; on the third day you shall go up to the house of the Lord.**
Malachi 4:2	But for you who revere my name **the sun of righteousness shall rise with healing in his wings. You shall go out leaping like calves from the stall.**
Peter 1 2:24	He himself bore our sins in his body on the cross, so that we might die to sins and live for righteousness; **by his wounds you have been healed.**
Proverbs 16:24	**Gracious words are like a honeycomb, sweetness to the soul and health to the body.**
Proverbs 17:22	**A cheerful heart is good medicine**, but a crushed spirit dries up the bones.
Proverbs 4:20-22	My son, pay attention to what I say; turn your ear to my words. Do not let them out of your sight, keep them

	within your heart; for they are life to those who find them and **health to one's whole body**.
Psalm 103:1-5	Praise the Lord, my soul; all my inmost being, praise his holy name. Praise the Lord, my soul, and forget not all his benefits—**who forgives all your sins and heals all your diseases**, who redeems your life from the pit and crowns you with love and compassion, who satisfies your desires with good thing, **so that your youth is renewed like the eagle's**.
Psalm 103:2-4	Praise the LORD, my soul, and forget not all his benefits - **who forgives all your sins and heals all your diseases**, who redeems your life from the pit and crowns you with love and compassion.
Psalm 107:19-21	Then they cried to the LORD in their trouble, and he saved them from their distress. **He sent out his word and healed them; he rescued them from the grave.** Let them give thanks to the LORD for his unfailing love and his wonderful deeds for mankind.
Psalm 146:8 |NIV|	**The Lord gives sight to the blind, the Lord lifts up those who are bowed down**, the Lord loves the righteous.
Psalm 147:3	**He heals the brokenhearted and binds up their wounds.**
Psalm 30:2	**LORD my God, I called to you for help, and you healed me.**
Psalm 41:2-3	The LORD protects and preserves them— they are counted among the blessed in the land - he does not give them over to the desire of their foes. **The LORD sustains them on their sickbed and restores them from their bed of illness.**
Psalm 41:4	**I said, Have mercy on me, LORD and heal me**, for I have sinned against you.
Psalm 6:2	**Have mercy on me, LORD, for I am faint; heal me, LORD, for my bones are in agony.**

PROTECTION SCRIPTURES

All Scriptures in this section NIV unless otherwise noted

Reference	Scripture
Chronicles 2 7:14-15	If my people, who are called by my name, will humble themselves and pray and seek my face and turn from their wicked ways, then I will hear from heaven, and **I will forgive their sin and will heal their land.** Now my eyes will be open and my ears attentive to the prayers offered in this place.
Corinthians 2 4:8-9 BSB	**8 We are hard pressed on all sides, but not crushed; perplexed, but not in despair; 9 persecuted, but not forsaken; struck down, but not destroyed.**
Deuteronomy 20:4 BSB	**For the Lord your God is He who goes with you to fight for you against your enemies, to give you the victory.**
Deuteronomy 31:6	Be strong and courageous. Do not be afraid or terrified because of them, for **the Lord your God goes with you; he will never leave you nor forsake you.**
Ephesians 6:10-15	10 Finally, be strong in the Lord and in his mighty power. 11 Put on the full armor of God, so that you can take your stand against the devil's schemes. 12 For our struggle is not against flesh and blood, but against the rulers, against the authorities, against the powers of this dark world and against the spiritual forces of evil in the heavenly realms. 13 **Therefore put on the full armor of God, so that if the day of evil comes, you may be able to stand your ground, and after you have done everything, to stand.** 14 Stand firm then,

SHELTER FROM THE PLAGUE

	with the belt of truth buckled around your waist, with the breastplate of righteousness in place, 15 and with your feet fitted with the readiness that comes from the gospel of peace.
Ephesians 6:13 BSB	**Therefore take up the full armor of God, so that when the day of evil comes, you will be able to stand your ground, and having done everything, to stand.**
Exodus 14:13-14 NKJV	And Moses said to the people, **'Do not be afraid. Stand still, and see the salvation of the LORD, which He will accomplish for you today.** For the Egyptians whom you see today, you shall see again no more forever. **The LORD will fight for you, and you shall hold your peace.'**
Hebrews 13:6 NKJV	So we may boldly say: **'The LORD is my helper; I will not fear. What can man do to me?'**
Isaiah 1:17	**Learn to do right; seek justice. Defend the oppressed. Take up the cause of the fatherless; plead the case of the widow.**
Isaiah 33:2	LORD, be gracious to us; we long for you. **Be our strength every morning, our salvation in time of distress.**
Isaiah 40:29	**He gives strength to the weary and increases the power of the weak.**
Isaiah 41:10-12	**10 So do not fear, for I am with you; do not be dismayed, for I am your God. I will strengthen you and help you; I will uphold you with my righteous right hand. 11 All who rage against you will surely be ashamed and disgraced; those who oppose you will be as nothing and perish. 12 Though you search for your enemies, you will not find them. Those who wage war against you will be as nothing at all.**
Isaiah 43:2	**2 When you pass through the waters, I will be with you; and when you pass through the rivers, they will not sweep over you. When you walk through the fire, you will not be burned; the flames will not set you ablaze.**
Isaiah 46:4	Even to your old age and gray hairs I am he, **I am he who will sustain you. I have made you and I will**

	carry you; I will sustain you and I will rescue you.
Isaiah 54:17	**No weapon forged against you will prevail, and you will refute every tongue that accuses you.** This is the heritage of the servants of the Lord, and this is their vindication from me, declares the Lord.
John 10:28-30	28 *I give them eternal life, and they shall never perish; no one will snatch them out of my hand.* 29 My Father, who has given them to me, is greater than all; no one can snatch them out of my Father's hand. 30 I and the Father are one.
John 14:27	*Peace I leave with you; my peace I give you. I do not give to you as the world gives. Do not let your hearts be troubled and do not be afraid.*
Mark 9:23	Said Jesus, *Everything is possible for the one who believes.*
Matthew 11:28-30	*Come to me, all you who are weary and burdened, and I will give you rest. Take my yoke upon you and learn from me, for I am gentle and humble in heart, and you will find rest for your souls. For my yoke is easy and my burden is light.*
Nahum 1:7 BSB	**The LORD is good, a stronghold in the day of distress.** He cares for those who trust in Him.
Philippians 4:13	**I can do all this through Yeshua who gives me strength.**
Philippians 4:19	**And my God will meet all your needs according to the riches of his glory in Christ Jesus.**
Proverbs 18:10 BSB	**The name of the Lord is a strong tower; the righteous run into it and are safe.**
Proverbs 18:12	**Humility comes before honor.**
Proverbs 2:11	**11 Discretion will protect you, and understanding will guard you.**
Proverbs 20:22 NKJV	Do not say, 'I will recompense evil'; **wait for the LORD, and He will save you.**
Proverbs 29:25 NKJV	The fear of man brings a snare, but **whoever trusts in**

	the LORD shall be safe.
Proverbs 30:5	Every word of God is flawless; **he is a shield to those who take refuge in him.**
Proverbs 4:23	**Above all else, guard your heart, for everything you do flows from it.**
Proverbs 4:6	**6 Do not forsake wisdom, and she will protect you; love her, and she will watch over you.**
Psalm 118:6	**The Lord is with me; I will not be afraid. What can mere mortals do to me?**
Psalm 118:8	**It is better to take refuge in the Lord than to trust in people.**
Psalm 119:114	**You are my refuge and my shield; I have put my hope in your word.**
Psalm 12:5	**5 Because the poor are plundered and the needy groan, I will now arise, says the LORD. I will protect them from those who oppress them.**
Psalm 121	**1 I lift up my eyes to the mountains— where does my help come from? 2 My help comes from the LORD, the Maker of heaven and earth. 3 He will not let your foot slip— he who watches over you will not slumber; 4 indeed, he who watches over Israel will neither slumber nor sleep. 5 The LORD watches over you— the LORD is your shade at your right hand; 6 the sun will not harm you by day, nor the moon by night. 7 The LORD will keep you from all harm— he will watch over your life; 8 the LORD will watch over your coming and going both now and forevermore.**
Psalm 138:7	**Though I walk in the midst of trouble, You will preserve my life. You will stretch out Your hand against the wrath of my enemies. Your right hand will save me.**
Psalm 140:4	**4 Keep me safe, LORD, from the hands of the wicked; protect me from the violent, who devise ways to trip my feet.**
Psalm 145:19 NKJV	He will fulfill the desire of those who fear Him; **He also will hear their cry and save them.**

Psalm 16:1	Keep me safe, my God, for in you I take refuge.
Psalm 16:8	I keep my eyes always on the Lord. With him at my right hand, I will not be shaken.
Psalm 17:7-8 NKJV	Show Your marvelous lovingkindness by Your right hand, O You who save those who trust in You from those who rise up against them. Keep me as the apple of Your eye; hide me under the shadow of Your wings.
Psalm 17:8-10	8 Keep me as the apple of your eye; hide me in the shadow of your wings 9 from the wicked who are out to destroy me, from my mortal enemies who surround me. 10 They close up their callous hearts, and their mouths speak with arrogance.
Psalm 18:30	As for God, his way is perfect: The Lord's word is flawless; he shields all who take refuge in him.
Psalm 18:35-36	You make your saving help my shield, and your right hand sustains me; your help has made me great. You provide a broad path for my feet, so that my ankles do not give way.
Psalm 20:1	1 May the LORD answer you when you are in distress; may the name of the God of Jacob protect you.
Psalm 23	1 The LORD is my shepherd, I lack nothing. 2 He makes me lie down in green pastures, he leads me beside quiet waters, 3 he refreshes my soul. He guides me along the right paths for his name's sake. 4 Even though I walk through the darkest valley, I will fear no evil, for you are with me; your rod and your staff, they comfort me. 5 You prepare a table before me in the presence of my enemies. You anoint my head with oil; my cup overflows. 6 Surely your goodness and love will follow me all the days of my life, and I will dwell in the house of the LORD forever.
Psalm 3:3-5	3 But you, Lord, are a shield around me, my glory, the One who lifts my head high. 4 I call out to the Lord, and he answers me from his holy mountain. 5 I lie down and sleep; I wake again, because the Lord sustains me.

SHELTER FROM THE PLAGUE

Psalm 30:10-11	Hear, LORD, and be merciful to me; LORD, be my help. You turned my wailing into dancing; you removed my sackcloth and clothed me with joy.
Psalm 32:7	You are my hiding place; you will protect me from trouble and surround me with songs of deliverance.
Psalm 34:17-22	The righteous cry out, and the LORD hears them; he delivers them from all their troubles. The LORD is close to the brokenhearted and saves those who are crushed in spirit. The righteous person may have many troubles, but the LORD delivers him out of them all; he protects all his bones, not one of them will be broken. Evil will slay the wicked; the foes of the righteous will be condemned. The LORD will rescue his servants; no one who takes refuge in him will be condemned.
Psalm 34:6 NKJV	This poor man cried out, and the LORD heard him, and saved him out of all his troubles.
Psalm 34:7-9	7 The angel of the Lord encamps around those who fear him, and he delivers them. 8 Taste and see that the Lord is good; blessed is the one who takes refuge in him. 9 Fear the Lord, you his holy people, for those who fear him lack nothing.
Psalm 46:1	God is our refuge and strength, an ever-present help in trouble.
Psalm 5:11	11 But let all who take refuge in you be glad; let them ever sing for joy. Spread your protection over them, that those who love your name may rejoice in you.
Psalm 57:1	1 Have mercy on me, my God, have mercy on me, for in you I take refuge. I will take refuge in the shadow of your wings until the disaster has passed.
Psalm 57:3 NKJV	He shall send from heaven and save me. He reproaches the one who would swallow me up. God shall send forth His mercy and His truth.
Psalm 59:1	1 Deliver me from my enemies, O God; be my fortress against those who are attacking me.
Psalm 59:16	In the morning I will sing of your love; for you are my

	fortress, my refuge in times of trouble.
Psalm 72:4 NKJV	He will bring justice to the poor of the people; He will save the children of the needy, and will break in pieces the oppressor.
Psalm 73:26 NKJV	God is the strength of my heart and my portion forever.
Psalm 91	1 Whoever dwells in the shelter of the Most High will rest in the shadow of the Almighty. 2 I will say of the LORD, He is my refuge and my fortress, my God, in whom I trust. 3 Surely he will save you from the fowler's snare and from the deadly pestilence. 4 He will cover you with his feathers, and under his wings you will find refuge; his faithfulness will be your shield and rampart. 5 You will not fear the terror of night, nor the arrow that flies by day, 6 nor the pestilence that stalks in the darkness, nor the plague that destroys at midday. 7 A thousand may fall at your side, ten thousand at your right hand, but it will not come near you. 8 You will only observe with your eyes and see the punishment of the wicked. 9 If you say, The LORD is my refuge, and you make the Most High your dwelling, 10 no harm will overtake you, no disaster will come near your tent. 11 For he will command his angels concerning you to guard you in all your ways; 12 they will lift you up in their hands, so that you will not strike your foot against a stone. 13 You will tread on the lion and the cobra; you will trample the great lion and the serpent. 14 Because he loves me, says the LORD, I will rescue him; I will protect him, for he acknowledges my name. 15 He will call on me, and I will answer him; I will be with him in trouble, I will deliver him and honor him. 16 With long life I will satisfy him and show him my salvation.
Romans 8:31	What, then, shall we say in response to these things? If God is for us, who can be against us?
Romans 8:37 NKJV	Yet in all these things we are more than conquerors through Him who loved us.
Samuel 1 14:6 NKJV	Then Jonathan said to the young man who bore his armor, 'Come, let us go over to the garrison of these

	uncircumcised; it may be that the LORD will work for us. **For nothing restrains the LORD from saving by many or by few.'**
Samuel 2 22:3-4 NKJV	**The God of my strength, in whom I will trust; my shield and the horn of my salvation, my stronghold and my refuge; my Savior, You save me from violence. I will call upon the LORD, who is worthy to be praised; so shall I be saved from my enemies.**
Samuel 2 22:32	For who is God besides the Lord? And who is the Rock except our God?
Thessalonians 1 5:23-24	23 May God himself, the God of peace, sanctify you through and through. May your whole spirit, soul and body be kept blameless at the coming of our Lord Jesus Christ. 24 **The one who calls you is faithful, and he will do it.**
Thessalonians 2 3:3	**3 The Lord is faithful, and he will strengthen you and protect you from the evil one.**
Timothy 2 4:18-20	**The Lord will rescue me from every evil attack and will bring me safely to his heavenly kingdom. To him be glory for ever and ever.**
Zephaniah 3:17 NKJV	**The Lord your God in your midst, the Mighty One, will save you.** He will rejoice over you with gladness, He will quiet you with His love, He will rejoice over you with singing.

DELIVERANCE SCRIPTURES

All Scriptures in this section NIV unless otherwise noted

Reference	Scripture
Acts 12:5-7	Peter was kept in prison, but the church was earnestly praying to God for him. The night before Herod was to bring him to trial, Peter was sleeping between two soldiers, bound with two chains, and sentries stood guard at the entrance. Suddenly an angel of the Lord appeared and a light shone in the cell. He struck Peter on the side and woke him up. "Quick, get up!" he said, and the chains fell off Peter's wrists.
Acts 16:26 BSB	Suddenly a strong earthquake shook the foundations of the prison. At once all the doors flew open, and everyone's chains came loose.
Acts 27:44 BSB	The rest were to follow on planks and various parts of the ship. In this way everyone was brought safely to land.
Acts 5:18-19 BSB	They arrested the apostles and put them in the public jail. But during the night an angel of the Lord opened the doors of the jail and brought them out.
Acts 7:25	Moses thought that his own people would realize that God was using him to rescue them, but they did not.
Chronicles 2 20:17	You will not have to fight this battle. Take up your positions; stand firm and see the deliverance the LORD will give you, Judah and Jerusalem. Do not be afraid; do not be discouraged. Go out to face them to-

	morrow, and the LORD will be with you.'
Chronicles 2 20:22 BSB	The moment they began their shouts and praises, the LORD set ambushes against the men of Ammon, Moab, and Mount Seir who had come against Judah, and they were defeated.
Corinthians 2 1:10	He has delivered us from such a deadly peril, and he will deliver us again. On him we have set our hope that he will continue to deliver us.
Daniel 3:27-29	The satraps, prefects, governors and royal advisers crowded around them. They saw that the fire had not harmed their bodies, nor was a hair of their heads singed; their robes were not scorched, and there was no smell of fire on them. "Praise be to the God of Shadrach, Meshach and Abednego, who has sent his angel and rescued his servants! For no other god can deliver in this way."
Daniel 6:22 BSB	My God sent His angel and shut the mouths of the lions. They have not hurt me, for I was found innocent in His sight.
Daniel 9:3 NKJV	Then I set my face toward the Lord God to make request by prayer and supplications, with fasting, sackcloth, and ashes.
Deuteronomy 32:36 BSB	For the LORD will vindicate His people and will have compassion on His servants.
Esther 4:14 BSB	For if you remain silent at this time, relief and deliverance for the Jews will arise from another place, but you and your father's house will perish. And who knows if perhaps you have come to the kingdom for such a time as this?
Esther 9:22 BSB	Because on those days the Jews gained rest from their enemies and the month in which their sorrow turned to joy and their mourning into a holiday. He wrote that these were to be days of feasting and joy, of sending gifts to one another and to the poor.
Exodus 12:42 NKJV	It is a night of solemn observance to the LORD for bringing them out of the land of Egypt. This is that night of the LORD, a solemn observance for all the

	children of Israel throughout their generations.
Exodus 13:3 BSB	So Moses told the people, "Remember this day, the day you came out of Egypt, out of the house of slavery For the LORD brought you out of it by the strength of His hand."
Exodus 14:13 BSB	Moses told the people, "Do not be afraid. Stand firm and you will see the LORD's salvation, which He will accomplish for you today; for the Egyptians you see today, you will never see again.
Exodus 14:30 BSB	That day the LORD saved Israel from the hand of the Egyptians.
Exodus 15:1 NKJV	Then Moses and the children of Israel sang this song to the LORD, and spoke, saying: "I will sing to the LORD, For He has triumphed gloriously! The horse and its rider He has thrown into the sea!
Galatians 1:4	Who gave Himself for our sins so that He might rescue us from this present evil age, according to the will of our God and Father.
Genesis 19:16	When he hesitated, the men grasped his hand and the hands of his wife and of his two daughters and led them safely out of the city, for the LORD was merciful to them.
Genesis 45:7 NKJV	God sent me before you to preserve a posterity for you in the earth, and to save your lives by a great deliverance.
Isaiah 43:13	Yes, and from ancient days I am he. No one can deliver out of my hand. When I act, who can reverse it?
Isaiah 46:4	Even to your old age and gray hairs I am he, I am he who will sustain you. I have made you and I will carry you; I will sustain you and I will rescue you.
Isaiah 6:7	With it he touched my mouth and said, "See, this has touched your lips; your guilt is taken away and your sin atoned for."
Isaiah 9:2	The people walking in darkness have seen a great light; on those living in the land of deep darkness a

	light has dawned.
Jeremiah 15:21 BSB	I will deliver you from the hand of the wicked and redeem you from the grasp of the ruthless.
Job 5:19 NKJV	He shall deliver you from six troubles, Yes, even in seven no evil shall touch you.
Joel 2:32 BSB	And everyone who calls on the name of the LORD will be saved; for on Mount Zion and in Jerusalem there will be deliverance, as the LORD has promised, among the remnant called by the LORD."
John 1 2:2 BSB	He Himself is the atoning sacrifice for our sins, and not only for ours but also for the sins of the whole world.
Luke 21:28	But when these things begin to take place, straighten up and lift up your heads, because your redemption is drawing near.
Matthew 1:21	She will give birth to a son, and you are to give him the name Yeshua, because he will save his people from their sins.
Philippians 1:19	For I know that through your prayers and God's provision of the Spirit of Jesus Christ what has happened to me will turn out for my deliverance.
Proverbs 10:2 BSB	Ill-gotten treasures profit nothing, but righteousness brings deliverance from death.
Proverbs 11:4 NKJV	Riches do not profit in the day of wrath, But righteousness delivers from death.
Proverbs 11:8-9	The righteous person is rescued from trouble, and... through knowledge the righteous escape.
Proverbs 14:25	A truthful witness saves lives
Proverbs 2:10-12	For wisdom will enter your heart snd knowledge will be pleasant to your soul. Discretion will guard you. Understanding will watch over you, to deliver you from the way of evil, from the man who speaks perverse things.
Proverbs 21:31 NKJV	The horse is prepared for the day of battle, But deliv-

	erance comes from the LORD.
Proverbs 28:26 BSB	He who trusts in himself is a fool, but one who walks in wisdom will be safe.
Psalm 108:12 NKJV	Give us help from trouble, For the help of man is useless.
Psalm 116:8 NKJV	For You have delivered my soul from death, My eyes from tears, And my feet from falling.
Psalm 124:6	Praise be to the LORD, who has not let us be torn by their anger.
Psalm 14:7 BSB	Oh, that the salvation of Israel would come from Zion! When the LORD restores His captive people, let Jacob rejoice, let Israel be glad!
Psalm 143:9 NKJV	Deliver me, O LORD, from my enemies (including plague). In You I take shelter.
Psalm 144:1-2	Blessed be the Lord my Rock, who trains my hands for war, my fingers for battle. He is my loving God and my fortress, my stronghold and my deliverer, my shield, in whom I take refuge,
Psalm 18:2 NKJV	The LORD is my rock and my fortress and my deliverer; My God, my strength, in whom I will trust; My shield and the horn of my salvation, my stronghold.
Psalm 22:21	Rescue me from the mouth of the lions; save me from the horns of the wild oxen.
Psalm 25:20	Guard my life and rescue me; do not let me be put to shame, for I take refuge in you.
Psalm 3:1-8	Lord, how many are my foes! How many rise up against me! But you, Lord, are a shield around me, my glory, the One who lifts my head high. I call out to the Lord, and he answers me from his holy mountain. I lie down and sleep. I wake again, because the Lord sustains me. I will not fear though tens of thousands assail me on every side. Arise, Lord! Deliver me, my God! From the Lord comes deliverance. May your blessing be on your people.
Psalm 34:19-20	The righteous person may have many troubles, but

	the Lord delivers him from them all. He protects all his bones, not one of them will be broken.
Psalm 40:1-3	I waited patiently for the Lord. He turned to me and heard my cry. He lifted me out of the pit, out of the mud and mire. He set my feet on a rock and gave me a firm place to stand. He put a new song in my mouth, a hymn of praise to our God. Many will see and fear the Lord and put their trust in him.
Psalm 40:17	But as for me, I am poor and needy. May the Lord think of me. You are my help and my deliverer. You are my God, do not delay.
Psalm 42:8 NKJV	The LORD will command His lovingkindness in the daytime, and in the night His song shall be with me — A prayer to the God of my life.
Psalm 43:1 BSB	Vindicate me, O God, and plead my case against ungodly people. Deliver me from deceitful and unjust men.
Psalm 44:4 NKJV	You are my King. O God, command victories for Israel. [all believers have been brought into Israel]
Psalm 50:15 NKJV	Call upon Me in the day of trouble; I will deliver you, and you shall glorify Me."
Psalm 59:2 NKJV	Deliver me from the workers of iniquity.
Psalm 60:11 BSB	Give us deliverance from the enemy, for the help of man is worthless.
Psalm 71:4 NKJV	Deliver me, O my God, out of the hand of the wicked, Out of the hand of the unrighteous and cruel man.
Psalm 72:4 NKJV	He will bring justice to the poor of the people; He will save the children of the needy, And will break in pieces the oppressor.
Psalm 74:12	But God is my King from long ago; he brings salvation on the earth.
Psalm 77:11	I will remember the deeds of the LORD; yes, I will remember your miracles of long ago.
Psalm 91:3	**For it is He who delivers you from the snare of the trapper And from the deadly pestilence.**

Samuel 1 17:37 BSB	And David said, "The LORD, who delivered me from the mouth of the lion and the claws of the bear, will deliver me from the hand of this Philistine."
Samuel 1 2:1 BSB	At that time Hannah prayed: "My heart rejoices in the LORD in whom my cause is exalted. My mouth speaks boldly against my enemies, for I rejoice in Your salvation."
Samuel 2 22:1-2 BSB	David sang this song to the LORD on the day the LORD had delivered him from the hand of all his enemies and from the hand of Saul. He said: "The LORD is my rock, and my fortress, and my deliverer."
Thessalonians 2 3:2 NKJV	We pray that we may be delivered from unreasonable and wicked men.